The Rise of Marcion and the Fall of the Faithful

by: Jeff E. Brannon

THE RISE OF MARCION AND THE FALL OF THE FAITHFUL

by:
JEFF E. BRANNON

The Rise of Marcion and the Fall of the Faithful
Copyright © 2025 by Jeff E. Brannon
All rights reserved.

Printed in the USA.
ISBN-13: 978-1-969004-02-5
ISBN-10: 978-1-969004-02-5

Proof Productions

Moundsville, WV 26041

@2025 by Jeff Brannon

All Rights Reserved. Published 2025

Cover art by Jeff E. Brannon.

No part of this book may be used or reproduced in any manner whatsoever without written permission except in the case of brief quotations embodied in critical articles and reviews. For information contact:

TheWayRemnant@gmail.com

The King James Version (KJV) & (KVJ 1611) used in this book is used by public domain in the United States.

Some of the Scriptures contained herein are from THE HOLY BIBLE, NEW LIVING TRANSLATION (NLT) Copyright 1996, 2004, 2007 by Tyndale House Foundation. Used by permission of Tyndale House Publishers Inc., Carol Stream, Illinois 60188. All rights reserved.

Some of the Scriptures contained herein are from The Septuagint version of the Old Testament Copyright 1971 by Zondervan Publishing House. Used by permission. All rights reserved.

SCRIPTURES, TREE OF LIFE VERSION (TLV) Copyright 2014, 2016 by the Tree of Life Bible Society. Used by permission. All rights reserved.

All images in this work are either public domain, taken from Wikimedia Commons, CC-BY-SA-3.0 and/or are original creations by Jeff Brannon. Every effort has been made to comply with copyright laws, but there may be cases where we have made a mistake. If so, the publisher will be happy to correct any omission of credit and/or replace/remove content as needed in future printing

Acknowledgements

Certain voices stood with me while I wrote this, offering strength, patience, and prayer when the path felt narrow and demanding.
Often the work required late hours and long study, but I never walked alone.
My gratitude extends first to the Father, whose wisdom guided every page.
Every insight, correction, and conviction came from Him.

Others poured encouragement into this project when doubt rose like a tide.
Unwavering support from family and friends reminded me that truth is always worth pursuit.
Those who challenged assumptions became unexpected allies in sharpening the message.

Over time I learned that history does not hide forever. It waits for eyes willing to see.
Faithful brothers and sisters helped uncover sources, manuscripts, and forgotten testimony.

Historic voices ancient and modern, whether agreement or resistance, pushed this work deeper.
Even disagreement proved valuable, pressing research to be honest and thorough.
Respect belongs to every scholar whose work I leaned on for clarity and contrast.

Miranda, my steadfast partner, carried peace into long writing nights and asked the questions that mattered most.
Your quiet strength gave this book more shape than you realize.

Pastors, teachers, and readers who encouraged me forward, thank you.
Every conversation, every prayer, every shared resource mattered.
Only through community does truth stand firm against centuries of tradition.
People who hunger for Scripture itself are the reason this work exists.
Let each page serve as a call to examine, to test, and to return to the foundation.
Eternity weighs truth more heavily than comfort. I offer these pages in that light.

To our audience on The Way Remnant YouTube channel, thank you for walking with us, thinking with us, and pursuing truth with courage. Your hunger for understanding keeps the fire lit.

(did you find it?)

Dedication

For every believer who felt the weight of tradition press against conviction.
You kept reading.
You kept praying.
You kept digging when others said the answers were already settled.
May these pages strengthen your courage to stand.

An Invitation to the Reader

Before you begin, I want to speak to you plainly.

This book is not only written to inform or challenge you. It is written because the Father is still calling people into covenant with Him. If you are reading this and sense a pull toward truth, toward repentance, or toward something deeper than religion, that matters.

From the beginning, Yehovah has desired relationship, not distance. Covenant has always been His way of restoring what was broken. When humanity turned away, He did not abandon us. He prepared a way back.

That way is Yeshua.

Through His obedience, His sacrifice, and His resurrection, reconciliation with the Father was made possible. Sin no longer has to define you. Separation does not have to be your future. Through Yeshua, forgiveness is real, restoration is offered, and new life can begin.

If you have never entered into covenant with the Father, you can begin now. Speak to Him honestly. Confess what you know is sin. Turn from it. Acknowledge Yeshua as the one sent by the Father to restore what was lost. Ask to be filled with His Spirit and taught His ways.

A Prayer to Begin Covenant

Father Yehovah,

I come to You honestly and without excuses.
I confess my sin and the ways I have walked apart from You.
I turn from those paths and ask for Your forgiveness.

I acknowledge Yeshua as the One You sent,
the Messiah through whom restoration and life are made possible.
Because of Him, I ask to be cleansed and brought back into covenant with You.

Fill me with Your Spirit.
Teach me Your ways.
Give me a heart that desires truth, obedience, and faithfulness.
Strengthen me to walk the path You have set before me.

I place my life in Your hands and ask You to begin Your work in me.
Let what is broken be restored, and let what is dead be made alive.

In Yeshua's name - Amen.

Welcome to the Kingdom of Yehovah. Through covenant in Yeshua, you are no longer separated but brought near and called to serve as part of a Kingdom of priests, set apart to walk in truth and obedience. Walk forward with confidence, knowing the Father is faithful to teach you His ways and complete the work He has begun in you.

Foreword

This is the book I wish I had in my hands nine years ago, back when I experienced a major crossroads in my walk with God. Being raised up in a nominal Christian household as a "gentile", I finally made a firm commitment to Christ at the age of 16. But after eight solid years into my faith journey, things just didn't add up. Going on missionary trips, attending a four-year Christian college, sitting through hundreds of church services, leading worship—no matter what I did, I just could not seem to satisfy that spiritual thirst within the essence of my being. I longed for the authentic Christian experience I always read about in the book of Acts. The early church's miraculous accounts of holiness and supernatural intimacy with God were so real to me, yet so far away. It didn't matter where I looked for answers, either. Pentecostal and charismatic churches weren't the answer, just like the Calvary Chapel and Baptist churches I grew up attending. Something was missing, which is why I had no choice but to make the difficult decision to walk away from it all. Not only did I refuse to live a lie, but deep down, I knew whatever that one missing thing was, it was out there. I just needed to intentionally isolate from the cultural distractions and traditions that were preventing me from hearing God's voice. Thankfully, my wife also wholeheartedly joined me in this investigation for the truth. Then, in 2016, my wife and I kept our very first Sabbath together as non-Jewish Christians. That one simple act changed everything.

Walking in God's ancient path, or The Way, comes from a place of deep conviction and true courage. It takes determination to step away from the comfort and familiarity of how we were all taught to follow God within the parameters of Western Christianity. All our lives, we were told: "Keeping God's Law is legalism. The Torah was nailed to the cross and done away with. That's for Jews, anyways. The Law is actually a yoke of bondage. Even worse, you are trampling underfoot the blood of Christ by attempting to keep the 'Old Covenant'. You have fallen from grace!". From Catholicism to Protestantism, this all-too-familiar consensus on God's Law has been faithfully proclaimed for many centuries now. But, why exactly are these sentiments towards God's very own Word so pervasive and unanimous across virtually every denomination of Christianity? Where did this strange animosity towards the first five books of the Bible actually originate from? Why are Christians so convinced that obedience to God's instructions is subjective and entirely optional? Well, wonder no more. The analysis that Jeff Brannon presents in this intriguing book on heresiology will finally leave you with so many of the answers you have been looking for but haven't been able to find. It's time to rediscover authentic Christianity, exactly how Jesus Himself demonstrated it.

Unlike other popular works that have addressed the subject of heresy, Jeff carefully defines "The Way" that Jesus taught and practiced without letting 21st-century biases or seeker-friendly pandering corrupt the simplicity of the matter. This perspective is absolutely essential. By defining the Torah as the ultimate foundation for the faith and practice of first century saints, Jeff is able to reveal the very essence of heresy while expertly judging the degree to which ancient false teachings still manage to affect the Church to this day. Without this Torah-centric perspective, understanding the roots of heresy, and its modern-day fruits, is impossible. With so many people now caught in the crossfire of compromise, falsehood, and outright licentiousness, the message in this book is not simply a well-researched, methodical, and scholarly presentation—though it certainly is—but it also presents an opportunity for God's people to recognize the real extent of the lies they have inherited. It presents an opportunity to worship God in an intellectually honest way that acknowledges just how far modern Christianity has indeed fallen. This book ushers the reader into a unique opportunity for authentic repentance. Your only job right now is to choose to approach this text with a humble heart and an open mind, and you will be rewarded. Whether you're a new Christian or you've been walking with God for a while, Jeff's presentation, embedded with tools like reflection questions and prayers, offers sobering moments of growth and discipleship. Prepare to be challenged, and may Yehovah bless you as you take up your cross and walk in obedience to Him.

— Abraham Ojeda, author of *Bible Prophecy Secrets*

Table of Contents

Preface 1
Part 1 The Root of Heresy 8
   Chapter 1 The Seeds of Deception 9
   Chapter 2 Simon Magus: Power Without Purity 14
   Chapter 3 Nicolas and the Spirit of Compromise 20
   Chapter 4 Cerinthus and the Counter Gospel 27
   Chapter 5 Valentinus and the System of Secret Knowledge 37
   Chapter 6 Marcion and the Great Divide 45
Part 2 Heresies Revived 56
   Chapter 7 The Heresy That Never Died 57
   Chapter 8 Gnosticism in the Pulpit 64
   Chapter 9 Grace Without Holiness 70
   Chapter 10 Cerinthus Reborn: A Reduced Christ 77
   Chapter 11 Marcion's Bible in the Modern Church 84
   Chapter 12 The Great Disconnect 95
Part 3 The Return of the Faithful 107
   Chapter 13 Come Out of Her, My People 108
   Chapter 14 Testing the Doctrine 113
   Chapter 15 Returning to the Ancient Path 119
   Chapter 16 Walking in the Way 124
   Chapter 17 Renouncing the Lies 128

Chapter 18 The Faithful Remnant 134

Part 4 Restoring the Foundations 140

Chapter 19 Yehovah's Compassion in the Hebrew Scriptures
.... 148

Chapter 20 The Rejection of the Written Torah 1488

Chapter 21 Denying the Hebrew Roots of the Gospel 15555

Chapter 22 Attacks on Gospel Authorship 16363

Chapter 23 The False Divide Between Law and Grace 2077

Chapter 24 Denial of Yeshua's True Identity 23434

Chapter 25 Gnosticism and Dualism 24040

Chapter 26 Subversion of Canon 2466

Chapter 27 Severing the Apostles from Their Jewish Context
.... 25353

Chapter 28 Spiritual Elitism and Secret Knowledge 2599

Chapter 29 Misused Scriptures Explained in Context 2677

Chapter 30 Marcion in New Clothes: A Rebuttal to
Dispensationalism 28484

About The Author 300

A Word from the Publisher 31212

THE RISE OF MARCION AND THE FALL OF THE FAITHFUL

Preface

Yeshua once warned, "Many false prophets will rise up and deceive many" (*Matthew 24:11, NLT*).
Those words were not spoken only for His disciples two thousand years ago. They were spoken for us.

Every generation faces the same test. Will we hold fast to what Yehovah said, or will we let the culture and clever voices twist truth until it loses its shape? History shows that deception rarely walks in wearing horns. It walks in quoting Scripture, just slightly out of tune.

That is how heresy works. It sounds close enough to truth that only those grounded in the Word recognize the difference.

Why This Book Exists

This book was born from both grief and hope.
Grief, because I watched the modern Church repeat the same mistakes the early believers fought so hard to correct. Hope, because Yehovah still calls out a remnant who hunger for truth more than tradition.

The story of heresy did not begin in the Middle Ages or in the Enlightenment. It began in the very days when the ink of the New Testament was still wet. As the apostles preached the gospel, others rose up beside them with new ideas and revelations that mixed the Word of God with pride and philosophy.

THE RISE OF MARCION AND THE FALL OF THE FAITHFUL

Some claimed deeper knowledge.
Some twisted grace into license.
Some separated the God of Israel from the Father of Yeshua.

Though time has passed, those same ideas live on. They have simply changed clothes and taken new pulpits.

This book exists to trace that line from its roots to its fruits, from Simon Magus to Marcion, and from Marcion to the modern Church. It exists to help us see what happened, where we went wrong, and how to return.

A Pastor's Awakening

I did not write this book as an outsider looking in.
For years I served as a minister and pastor who loved God deeply and cared for His people with all my heart. I preached salvation by grace through faith. I taught the Scriptures with passion. But over time, something began to stir in me.

I could not reconcile the Church I saw in the book of Acts with the one I saw around me. The power, unity, and holiness that marked the early believers seemed absent. We had theology, but little transformation. We had programs, but little presence.

As I dug deeper into the Word, I began to uncover how much we had inherited from traditions that did not come from the apostles at all. I found doctrines that sounded biblical but had roots in the very heresies the early Church fought to expose.

It did not come all at once. It came slowly, like the rising of the dawn, clearing the fog one ray of light at a time. Each discovery

THE RISE OF MARCION AND THE FALL OF THE FAITHFUL

brought both revelation and grief. I realized how far the modern Church had drifted from the foundation the apostles laid.

There was a cost. Pursuing truth always costs something. I lost lifelong friendships and ministry acquaintances who could not understand why I no longer fit into their systems. But Yehovah, in His mercy, restored me many times over. He gave me new peace, new purpose, and new brothers and sisters who love truth more than comfort. Like Job, I can say that what I have now is far greater than what I lost.

The Forgotten Faith

Before the term "Christian" ever existed, believers were called followers of *The Way*. They followed Yeshua's example of obedience, love, and holiness. They saw Torah as the foundation of a righteous life, not as bondage. They celebrated the feasts of Yehovah with joy. They worshiped in the Spirit and walked in truth.

Their faith was both Spirit-filled and Torah-embracing. It was not a religion of rules, but a relationship grounded in covenant.

Somewhere along the way, that identity was replaced. *The Way* became *Christianity,* and over time Christianity drifted. The separation from Israel deepened. The Law was called legalism. The feasts were called Jewish. The commandments were treated as optional. The Church built new foundations and called them old ones.

This book seeks to recover that original vision, not by starting a new movement, but by returning to the ancient path that Yeshua and His disciples walked.

THE RISE OF MARCION AND THE FALL OF THE FAITHFUL

The Ripple Effect of Heresy

Simon Magus offered the apostles money to buy the power of the Holy Spirit. Nicolas preached liberty without holiness. Cerinthus denied that the God of the Old Testament was the same as the Father of Yeshua. Valentinus taught that salvation came through secret knowledge.

Then came Marcion, who gathered all these errors into one system. He rejected the Old Testament, rewrote the New, and painted the God of Israel as cruel and inferior.

The early fathers stood against him with courage and conviction. Yet somehow, many of his ideas survived.

When churches teach that the Old Testament no longer applies, that the Church has replaced Israel, that obedience is legalism, or that revelation can outrun Scripture, they repeat the same ancient errors that once tore the faith apart.

This is not ancient history. It is our present reality.

The Modern Mirror

Today, Simon Magus lives on in ministries that equate blessing with money. Nicolas lives on in the message of grace without repentance. Cerinthus lives on in those who reduce Yeshua to a moral reformer. Valentinus lives on in those who exalt personal revelation above Scripture. And Marcion lives on in pulpits that teach believers to unhitch their faith from the Old Testament.

Different names. Same spirit.

THE RISE OF MARCION AND THE FALL OF THE FAITHFUL

We have built our theology with borrowed bricks and wondered why the house keeps cracking.

This book is not written to condemn but to expose. It is a call to hold up every doctrine to the light of Scripture and ask, "Did this come from the apostles, or from the men who opposed them?"

Why It Matters Now

We live in a time when truth is being rewritten and the gospel is being reshaped to fit human preference. The modern Church has become skilled at comforting people, but hesitant to confront sin. We call rebellion authenticity. We call lawlessness freedom. We call partial truth grace.

But truth has never changed. Yeshua did not come to abolish the Torah or the prophets, but to fulfill them. He is the Word made flesh, not the cancellation of it.

If we remove the foundation, the house cannot stand. If we cut ourselves off from the root, the branch withers. The only way forward is to return to what is written.

This message matters because the age of compromise is ending. Yehovah is raising a people who will no longer settle for half-truths. He is calling His Church to awaken, to repent, and to walk once again in the power of the Spirit and the truth of His Word.

What This Book Will Do

This book unfolds in four parts.

THE RISE OF MARCION AND THE FALL OF THE FAITHFUL

The first traces the rise of heresy from Simon Magus to Marcion, showing how deception took root in the first generations of believers.

The second reveals how those same errors have reemerged in the modern Church and continue to shape doctrine, worship, and identity.

The third is a call to return. It offers practical tools, prayers, and a scriptural checklist to help believers come out of deception and walk again in the faith of *The Way*.

The fourth part brings everything together. It gathers the research, the history, and the warnings from the earlier chapters and lays them out in one clear foundation. It walks through the key Scriptures people misuse, exposes the doctrines that grew out of Marcion's influence, and shows how the apostles actually understood faith, grace, and obedience. This section is meant to steady your footing. It gives you the tools to discern truth, answer common objections, and stand firm when others drift.

Every page is built on one truth. The same Yehovah who spoke through Moses and the prophets is the One who walked among us as Yeshua the Messiah. His Word has not changed. His covenant has not failed. And His call still echoes, "Come out of her, My people."

A Pastoral Challenge and Promise

If you read this book with an open heart, you may find some of your beliefs challenged. That is not meant to offend but to awaken. Truth does not fear inspection. It invites it.

THE RISE OF MARCION AND THE FALL OF THE FAITHFUL

Do not read to argue. Read to understand. Take notes. Study the Scriptures. Read the writings of the early fathers. Ask the Holy Spirit to confirm what is true and expose what is not.

If you seek truth with humility, you will find it. Yehovah never hides from a sincere heart.

My hope is that this journey rekindles your love for Scripture, renews your reverence for the commandments of God, and fills you with the joy of knowing that grace and obedience were never meant to be enemies. They were meant to walk hand in hand.

We are living in days of shaking. Only what is rooted in truth will endure. Those who build on the rock of Yeshua's words will stand when the winds of deception blow.

The time for shallow religion is over. The time for faithful obedience has come.

May this book open your eyes to see the patterns of deception that have crept into the faith, but more than that, may it lead you to the joy of walking once again in the ancient paths where grace and truth meet.

And when the world grows dark, may you stand among the faithful who shine with the light of Yehovah's truth until the day Yeshua returns.

With humility and hope,
 Jeff E. Brannon

THE RISE OF MARCION AND THE FALL OF THE FAITHFUL

Part 1 The Root of Heresy

Every story has a beginning, even the story of deception. Long before modern doctrines blurred the lines of truth, the early Church fought spiritual battles that shaped the faith we inherited. The apostles did not minister in a quiet age. They contended for the Gospel from the very start.

Part 1 takes you back to those early days. Here you will see how the first fractures formed, how false teachers rose within the community of believers, and how ideas foreign to Scripture tried to pull the Church away from the faith once delivered. You will follow the trail from Simon Magus to Marcion and watch how confusion spread when men traded obedience for innovation and revelation for speculation.

This section will show you:

- How heresy entered the Church during the days of the apostles
- How false teachers twisted grace and rejected the Torah
- How early leaders confronted deception with courage
- How the seeds of later error were planted in the first century

Most of all, you will see that the battle for truth is not new. The apostles faced it. The early Church faced it. And their responses still guide us today.

This is where the story begins.

Chapter 1 The Seeds of Deception

The Master's Warning

Before we talk about history or heresy, we need to start with the words of Yeshua Himself. He did not leave us guessing about what would happen in the generations after Him. He said,

"Don't let anyone mislead you, for many will come in my name, claiming, 'I am the Messiah.' They will deceive many" (Matthew 24:4–5, NLT).

A few verses later He added,

"Many false prophets will appear and will deceive many people. Sin will be rampant everywhere, and the love of many will grow cold" (Matthew 24:11–12, NLT).

When you read those words, it is easy to think He was only talking about the end times, about some future deception that is still on its way. But those words started coming true almost immediately after He ascended. The apostles did not have to look centuries ahead. They lived through the beginnings of it. They saw the early seeds of false teaching already growing inside the young church.

The Warning Within the Church

When Paul met with the elders from Ephesus for the last time, his words must have landed heavy. He said,

"I know that false teachers, like vicious wolves, will come in among you after I leave, not sparing the flock. Even some men from your

THE RISE OF MARCION AND THE FALL OF THE FAITHFUL

own group will rise up and distort the truth in order to draw a following" (Acts 20:29–30, NLT).

Think about that for a moment. He was not warning about outsiders. He said some from your own group. That means deception often does not walk through the front door wearing a name tag that says *false prophet*. It grows quietly among familiar faces.

Peter said the same thing:

"There were also false prophets in Israel, just as there will be false teachers among you. They will cleverly teach destructive heresies and even deny the Master who bought them" (2 Peter 2:1, NLT).

And Jude, Yeshua's half-brother, did not hold back either:

"Some ungodly people have wormed their way into your churches, saying that God's marvelous grace allows us to live immoral lives" (Jude 4, NLT).

If you and I had been sitting in one of those early house churches, we might have been surprised. But the apostles were not. They saw it coming. The biggest threat to the faith was never from the Roman Empire. It was from within the congregation, when believers started to twist the message to fit their own desires.

The First Signs of Trouble

John wrote, "You have heard that the Antichrist is coming, and already many such antichrists have appeared" (1 John 2:18, NLT). He was not talking about some end-time villain yet. He meant the spirit of deception was already present.

THE RISE OF MARCION AND THE FALL OF THE FAITHFUL

Paul noticed the same thing: "You happily put up with whatever anyone tells you, even if they preach a different Jesus" (2 Corinthians 11:4, NLT).

So even in the first generation there were two kinds of corruption beginning to form:

1. Moral corruption - people who wanted grace without repentance.

2. Philosophical corruption - teachers mixing Greek ideas and mystery religions with the message of Yeshua.

One distorted holiness. The other distorted truth. Both spread faster than the apostles could travel.

How the Apostles Responded

The apostles did not smooth things over for the sake of unity. They drew clear lines. John said, "Anyone who denies the Father and the Son is an antichrist" (1 John 2:22, NLT). That is strong language, but it came from love. It came from a shepherd guarding his flock.

Paul even confronted Peter to his face when compromise threatened the gospel (Galatians 2:11–14, NLT). He was not trying to embarrass him. He was protecting the truth.

Later, Irenaeus, one of the early church fathers who learned from the disciples of John, wrote that the apostles "knew through our Lord Jesus Christ that there would be strife about the name of the Lord, and therefore, foreseeing all, they delivered the truth to us."[1] Eusebius, another early historian, said, "Simon the Samaritan, whom the apostles refuted in the Acts, was the author of all heresy."[2]

They traced every later false doctrine back to those early seeds of rebellion in Acts 8. The infection started small, but it never stopped spreading.

Why the Seeds Matter

If the first believers faced deception inside their own gatherings, we can be sure we will face it too. The only safe place is the same one they found: holding tight to what the apostles actually taught. That is why Jude urged the Church to "defend the faith that God has entrusted once for all time to his holy people" (Jude 3, NLT).

This book will follow those early seeds of deception as they grow into full heresies: names like Simon Magus, Nicolas, Cerinthus, Valentinus, and Marcion. But as we walk through history, remember that Yeshua already told us it would happen.

Every false teaching, old or new, starts with one choice: to redefine Yehovah's Word to fit human will. Once that seed is planted, it grows fast unless someone uproots it.

THE RISE OF MARCION AND THE FALL OF THE FAITHFUL

Reflection Questions

1. When Yeshua warned about false Messiahs and prophets, what kind of deception do you think He meant?
2. How do Paul's and Peter's warnings show that deception can rise from inside the Church, not just outside?
3. What does it look like today when people try to reshape the Word of Yehovah to fit their lifestyle or tradition?

Key Scriptures (NLT)

- Matthew 24:4–5, 11–12
- Acts 20:28–30
- 2 Peter 2:1–3
- Jude 3–4
- 1 John 2:18–23

Primary Sources for Footnotes

1. Irenaeus, *Against Heresies*, Preface, in *Ante-Nicene Fathers*, Vol. 1 (Edinburgh: T&T Clark, 1885).
2. Eusebius, *Ecclesiastical History* 2.13.6, in *Nicene and Post-Nicene Fathers*, Vol. 1 (Grand Rapids: Eerdmans, 1955).

THE RISE OF MARCION AND THE FALL OF THE FAITHFUL

Chapter 2 Simon Magus: Power Without Purity

A Counterfeit Revival

If you were to walk through the streets of Samaria in the days of the apostles, you would hear people talking about a man named Simon. He was famous, admired, and feared all at once. The Book of Acts says that "for many years he had astounded the people of Samaria with his magic" (Acts 8:11, NLT).

When Philip came preaching about the Kingdom of God and the name of Yeshua the Messiah, something powerful happened. Crowds believed, demons fled, and the lame were healed. The city was filled with joy. Simon watched all this and wanted to be part of it. He followed Philip, amazed at the real miracles of the Holy Spirit.

At first, it looked like a revival. But underneath, something else was stirring. Simon wanted the power of God without the purity of heart that must come with it.

The Attempt to Purchase the Spirit

When the apostles Peter and John came to Samaria, they prayed for the new believers to receive the Holy Spirit. Scripture says,

"Then Peter and John laid their hands upon these believers, and they received the Holy Spirit" (Acts 8:17, NLT).

What happened next exposes Simon's heart.

THE RISE OF MARCION AND THE FALL OF THE FAITHFUL

"When Simon saw that the Spirit was given when the apostles laid their hands on people, he offered them money to buy this power" (Acts 8:18–19, NLT).

Peter's response was sharp and clear:

"May your money be destroyed with you for thinking God's gift can be bought. You can have no part in this, for your heart is not right with God" (Acts 8:20–21, NLT).

Simon wanted the supernatural without submission. He desired spiritual authority without repentance. That is the first recorded counterfeit of the Holy Spirit's power in Church history.

What We Really Know About Simon Magus

Many legends grew around Simon after Acts 8, but certain facts are repeated consistently by early writers. Here is what we can say with confidence.

1. He practiced sorcery before meeting Philip. Acts 8 calls him a man "who had astounded the people of Samaria with his magic" (NLT). His influence was spiritual, not merely illusion.
2. He believed and was baptized, but his heart was not right. He attached himself to the movement, but Peter's rebuke shows his motives were corrupt.
3. He tried to buy the power of the Holy Spirit. This act gave us the term *simony*, meaning the buying or selling of spiritual office.
4. He later claimed divine status. Justin Martyr wrote that Simon went to Rome and "was honored as a god" with a

statue labeled *Simoni Deo Sancto*-"To Simon the Holy God."[1]

5. He blended faith in Messiah with pagan philosophy. Irenaeus said Simon called himself "the Supreme Power" and taught that the visible world was created by angelic beings who rebelled against a higher god.[2]

6. He introduced a female companion named Helena, calling her the first Thought of God. This reflects early Gnostic ideas about emanations and divine pairs.[3]

7. He promised salvation through secret knowledge rather than repentance. Hippolytus said Simon taught that people carried a divine spark that could be awakened by knowing his teachings.[4]

These points give us a concise picture of Simon's doctrine. He was not simply a misguided convert; he became the prototype of Gnosticism. His message replaced relationship with revelation, holiness with hidden knowledge, and submission to Yehovah with worship of self.

Tracing Simon's Influence

According to the early writings, Simon did not fade quietly into history. Irenaeus wrote that he "pretended to be the Supreme Power" and that his followers called themselves *Simonians*.[5] They believed salvation came through special knowledge, a belief that later shaped Gnosticism.

Hippolytus described how Simon mixed biblical language with mystical ideas, teaching that the divine spark was trapped inside people and could be freed by secret knowledge.⁶ That same language would reappear in later heresies such as Valentinianism and even in Marcion's theology.

Every one of these movements shared Simon's DNA: pride, elitism, and a desire for control. It began with one man trying to buy the gift of God, and it spread into entire systems that replaced the Holy Spirit with human authority.

Power Without Purity

Simon Magus wanted power, but not the kind that transforms the heart. He wanted to be seen as great. Acts 8:9 says, "He boasted that he was someone great, and all the people, from the least to the greatest, often spoke of him as 'the Great One—the Power of God'" (NLT).

The early believers knew that the true Power of God was the Holy Spirit working through a surrendered life. Simon imitated that power but never submitted to its source.

Throughout history, whenever the Church has elevated giftedness above godliness, it has repeated Simon's mistake. The result is always the same: people are impressed, but heaven is grieved.

Why This Matters Now

We begin this journey with Simon because he represents the first fracture in the faith. Every heresy that followed (Nicolas, Cerinthus, Valentinus, and Marcion) echoed his pattern. Each wanted a version of faith that could be controlled or redefined.

THE RISE OF MARCION AND THE FALL OF THE FAITHFUL

Simon shows us what happens when the desire for recognition replaces the call to repentance. He reminds us that the greatest danger to the Church is not persecution but pride.

If we do not learn from his story, we risk repeating it. The true power of Yehovah cannot be purchased, performed, or pretended. It can only rest on a life that is surrendered.

Reflection Questions

1. What stands out most about Simon's teaching? His false view of power, his pride, or his counterfeit gospel?
2. How can we tell the difference between true spiritual power and imitation today?
3. What practical steps help us keep purity above platform?

Key Scriptures (NLT)

- Acts 8:9–24
- Matthew 7:22–23
- 2 Corinthians 4:7
- James 4:6–8

Primary Sources for Footnotes

THE RISE OF MARCION AND THE FALL OF THE FAITHFUL

1. Justin Martyr, *First Apology*, 26, in *Ante-Nicene Fathers*, Vol. 1 (Edinburgh: T&T Clark, 1885).

2. Irenaeus, *Against Heresies*, 1.23, in *Ante-Nicene Fathers*, Vol. 1 (Edinburgh: T&T Clark, 1885).

3. Ibid.

4. Hippolytus, *Refutation of All Heresies*, 6.1–2, in *Ante-Nicene Fathers*, Vol. 5 (Edinburgh: T&T Clark, 1886).

5. Irenaeus, *Against Heresies*, 1.23.

6. Hippolytus, *Refutation of All Heresies*, 6.1–2.

THE RISE OF MARCION AND THE FALL OF THE FAITHFUL

Chapter 3 Nicolas and the Spirit of Compromise

A Church That Lost Its First Love

In the Book of Revelation, Yeshua spoke to seven congregations in Asia Minor. To the church at Ephesus, He said something that should make every believer pause:

"I know all the things you do. I have seen your hard work and your patient endurance. I know you don't tolerate evil people. You have examined the claims of those who say they are apostles but are not. You have discovered they are liars. You have patiently suffered for me without quitting. But I have this complaint against you. You don't love me or each other as you did at first" (Revelation 2:2–4, NLT).

Ephesus was strong in doctrine but weak in devotion. They could spot false teachers but had lost tenderness toward the One they defended.
  Then Yeshua added a short but sobering statement:

"But this is in your favor: You hate the evil deeds of the Nicolaitans, just as I do" (Revelation 2:6, NLT).

The believers in Ephesus were still discerning. They rejected something called the "deeds of the Nicolaitans." Yet in Pergamum, only a few verses later, Yeshua said the opposite:

"You tolerate some among you whose teaching is like that of Balaam... In a similar way, you have some Nicolaitans among you who follow the same teaching" (Revelation 2:14–15, NLT).

So what was this teaching that Yeshua said He hated?

THE RISE OF MARCION AND THE FALL OF THE FAITHFUL

What We Really Know About Nicolas

Unlike Simon Magus, Nicolas does not have a long trail of legends surrounding him, but early writers give us a few solid facts.

1. He was one of the first seven deacons. Acts 6:5 lists "Nicolas of Antioch, a convert to the Jewish faith" among those chosen to serve. He began as a respected and Spirit-filled man.

2. His followers later twisted his name into a doctrine. Early writers say the "Nicolaitans" took his example and corrupted it, promoting compromise and indulgence.

3. Irenaeus said they "lead lives of unrestrained indulgence." They claimed freedom in Messiah meant freedom from moral restraint.[1]

4. Hippolytus connected them to immorality and idolatry. He wrote that they mixed pagan feasts with worship and encouraged sexual sin.[2]

5. A shocking claim circulated about Nicolas himself. Clement of Alexandria wrote that Nicolas, "being accused of jealousy by the apostles, brought forward his wife and permitted anyone who wished to marry her."[3] This, according to Clement, was Nicolas' attempt to prove his detachment from worldly passion. Later followers twisted this gesture into open sexual license, using it to justify immorality in the name of liberty.[4]

Whether or not Nicolas actually did this is debated. Some Church Fathers, like Clement, tried to defend his intentions as a misguided act of self-denial rather than genuine corruption.[5] Regardless, the

THE RISE OF MARCION AND THE FALL OF THE FAITHFUL

movement that bore his name became synonymous with sensual indulgence and spiritual compromise.

Possible Link to Simon Magus

Nicolas and Simon Magus lived during the same period of Church history, both active in the mid-first century. Scripture places Nicolas in the Jerusalem community (Acts 6) and Simon in Samaria (Acts 8). These regions were close enough that ideas could travel easily.

While Scripture never says they met, it is reasonable to wonder whether the kind of deception that marked Simon's life influenced Nicolas or his followers later on. Simon tried to blend spiritual power with self-promotion. The Nicolaitans blended spiritual freedom with worldliness. Both reduced holiness to preference.

No ancient record directly links them, so we can only treat this as speculation, not fact. Still, the similarity is striking. Both movements replaced purity with permission and obedience with indulgence. They represent two branches of the same root problem: a heart that wants the benefits of faith without surrender to Yehovah's authority.

The Spirit of Compromise

The Nicolaitan mindset was simple but deadly. It said, "You can belong to Yeshua and still live like the world." It separated belief from behavior.

The name *Nicolaitan* may even carry a clue. It comes from two Greek words: *nikao*, meaning "to conquer," and *laos*, meaning "the people." Together it could mean "to conquer the people" or "to rule over the people."

That captures both sides of the deception. It conquered people by leading them into sin, and it ruled over them by replacing Yehovah's holiness with man-made permission.

Jude warned about people who "use God's marvelous grace as an excuse for living immoral lives" (Jude 4, NLT). That is the heart of Nicolaitan doctrine. It promised freedom but produced bondage.

How Compromise Creeps In

No one wakes up one day and decides to reject holiness. Compromise usually begins small. It starts when believers stop guarding what enters their hearts and homes.
In Ephesus, the church rejected this teaching. In Pergamum, they tolerated it. In Thyatira, they eventually embraced it. By the time of Laodicea, compromise had become culture.

Yeshua warned that lukewarm faith disgusts Him. He said, "Since you are like lukewarm water, neither hot nor cold, I will spit you out of my mouth" (Revelation 3:16, NLT).
The lesson is clear. What one generation tolerates, the next will normalize.

The Power of Tolerance and the Loss of Truth

The Nicolaitans turned grace into a license for sin. They confused mercy with permission.
That same deception is alive today in the form of what many call *hyper-grace*. It teaches that repentance is unnecessary because

THE RISE OF MARCION AND THE FALL OF THE FAITHFUL

"God already forgave you." It says obedience to Yehovah's commands is "legalism."

But Yeshua never gave us grace to ignore the Father's Word. He gave us grace to walk in it.

Paul said, "Should we keep on sinning so that God can show us more and more of his wonderful grace? Of course not!" (Romans 6:1–2, NLT).

The true gospel calls us out of sin, not into comfort with it. The Nicolaitan spirit reverses that call. It trades holiness or keeping the law for popularity and truth for convenience.

Tracing Nicolas' Influence

Irenaeus said the Nicolaitans "are the forerunners of those who falsely claim that it is right to indulge in every lust."[6]

Hippolytus connected them to later Gnostic sects that viewed the body as evil and physical acts as meaningless. If the flesh was already corrupt, they reasoned, then sexual immorality could not harm the soul.[7]

That idea spread quickly. Cerinthus and other early teachers built on it, creating a religion of "knowledge without obedience."

By the second century, some Christian groups were attending pagan feasts and calling it outreach. Others adopted Roman festivals but gave them Christian names. The line between holiness and compromise blurred.

From that soil, new distortions grew, each one rooted in the same lie the Nicolaitans embraced: that Yehovah's grace excuses what His Word forbids.

THE RISE OF MARCION AND THE FALL OF THE FAITHFUL

Why This Matters Now

Nicolas reminds us that compromise does not always look evil. Sometimes it wears the smile of acceptance and calls itself love. But real love always leads to holiness. Yeshua did not die to make us comfortable in sin. He died to make us free from it.

The Church in our time faces the same decision as those in Ephesus and Pergamum. Will we hate the deeds of the Nicolaitans, or will we tolerate them? The answer will determine whether we stay pure or become polluted.

Reflection Questions

1. What does compromise look like in the modern Church, and how can we resist it?
2. Why do you think Yeshua said He hated the deeds of the Nicolaitans?
3. How can grace and law work together rather than against each other?

Key Scriptures (NLT)

- Acts 6:1–6
- Revelation 2:6, 14–16
- Romans 6:1–2
- Jude 4

THE RISE OF MARCION AND THE FALL OF THE FAITHFUL

Primary Sources for Footnotes

1. Irenaeus, *Against Heresies*, 1.26, in *Ante-Nicene Fathers*, Vol. 1 (Edinburgh: T&T Clark, 1885).

2. Hippolytus, *Refutation of All Heresies*, 7.24, in *Ante-Nicene Fathers*, Vol. 5 (Edinburgh: T&T Clark, 1886).

3. Clement of Alexandria, *Stromata*, 3.4, in *Ante-Nicene Fathers*, Vol. 2 (Edinburgh: T&T Clark, 1885).

4. Eusebius, *Ecclesiastical History*, 3.29, quoting Clement's defense of Nicolas, in *Nicene and Post-Nicene Fathers*, Vol. 1 (Grand Rapids: Eerdmans, 1955).

5. Clement of Alexandria, *Stromata*, 3.4.

6. Irenaeus, *Against Heresies*, 1.26.

7. Hippolytus, *Refutation of All Heresies*, 7.24.

Chapter 4 Cerinthus and the Counter Gospel

When Truth Meets Counterfeit

If you have ever held a counterfeit bill, you know the trick is not in making something entirely new. It is in making something close enough to pass as the real thing. That is what Cerinthus tried to do with the gospel.

He lived near the end of the first century, at the same time as the apostle John. By then, the message of Yeshua was spreading across Asia Minor, but so were distortions of it. Cerinthus used the vocabulary of faith while replacing its meaning. He spoke about Jesus and the Creator but redefined both in a way that fit Greek philosophy more than Hebrew truth.

A Clash with the Apostle John

Church tradition says that one day, John the apostle entered a public bathhouse in Ephesus. When he saw Cerinthus inside, he turned and ran out, saying, *"Let us flee, lest the building fall down, for Cerinthus, the enemy of the truth, is within."*[1]

Whether the story is literal or symbolic, it captures John's attitude perfectly. He could not stand to share the same space with a man who denied that Yeshua was Yehovah in flesh. John understood something many believers forget today: error about who Yeshua is always begins with error about who Yehovah is.

THE RISE OF MARCION AND THE FALL OF THE FAITHFUL

What We Really Know About Cerinthus

From early church sources, we can summarize Cerinthus' teaching with some certainty.

1. He denied that Yeshua and the Messiah were the same. Cerinthus taught that Jesus was an ordinary man, born naturally of Joseph and Mary, and that "the Christ" was a divine spirit that descended on Him at baptism but left before the crucifixion.[2]

2. He separated the divine from the human. He rejected the idea that the Eternal Word could take on real flesh.

3. He mixed Jewish law with mystical speculation. He accepted parts of the Torah but reinterpreted them through hidden allegories rather than obedience.[3]

4. He redefined the God of the Old Testament. Cerinthus said that the Creator who made heaven and earth was not the supreme God but a lesser power, an angelic being or "demiurge."[4]

5. He claimed the higher, invisible Father sent the Christ-spirit to correct the Creator's errors.[5]

This was more than doctrinal confusion. It was a complete reversal of the faith handed down through Israel. Cerinthus took the God of Abraham, Isaac, and Jacob, the God who spoke to Moses from the burning bush, and labeled Him as inferior.

THE RISE OF MARCION AND THE FALL OF THE FAITHFUL

How Cerinthus Viewed Yehovah

To understand how far Cerinthus strayed, we have to look at where he came from. Ancient sources record that he was educated in Alexandria, Egypt, the home of Gnosticism.[6] Alexandria was a melting pot of Jewish theology, Greek philosophy, and Egyptian mysticism. It was a place where scholars tried to blend the wisdom of Moses with the reasoning of Plato.

That environment shaped Cerinthus' worldview. He could not accept that the Creator of Genesis, the One who formed Adam and gave the Torah, was the same God revealed in Yeshua.

Influenced by Gnostic philosophy, he believed the visible world was flawed and that matter itself was corrupt. In his system, a pure, unknowable deity existed far above creation. Below that supreme being were layers of lesser divine beings or *aeons*, one of which accidentally created the material world.[7]

That lower being, he said, was the God of the Hebrews, Yehovah. He described Him as proud, ignorant, and unaware of the higher, hidden Father above Him.[8]
In other words, the God who thundered from Sinai and delivered the Ten Commandments was, in Cerinthus' eyes, not truly God at all but a mistaken angel who believed Himself to be the only deity.

This view allowed Cerinthus to reject the authority of the Torah and the prophets. If the Old Testament God was a lesser being, then His commandments could be dismissed or reinterpreted.
That same thinking appears again later in Marcion, who claimed the God of Israel was a harsh legal deity and the Father of Yeshua was a different, loving one. Cerinthus planted the seed that Marcion later cultivated.

THE RISE OF MARCION AND THE FALL OF THE FAITHFUL

Why John's Gospel Confronts Him

John begins his Gospel with words that strike at the heart of Cerinthus' teaching:

"In the beginning the Word already existed. The Word was with God, and the Word was God. He existed in the beginning with God. God created everything through him, and nothing was created except through him" (John 1:1–3, NLT).

Those lines are not abstract poetry. They are theological warfare. John was saying, *Yeshua is the very Creator you deny.*
The One who spoke the universe into existence is the same One who walked among us. There is no lesser god, no chain of divine beings, no confusion between the God of Israel and the Christ of the New Covenant. They are one and the same.

John later wrote, "Anyone who denies that Jesus is the Christ has become an antichrist. Anyone who denies the Father and the Son is an antichrist" (1 John 2:22, NLT). That statement directly targets Cerinthus' two-God theology.

A Faith That Fit Human Philosophy

Cerinthus' ideas sounded intelligent to people trained in Greek philosophy. He made the faith seem more sophisticated. He allowed the intellectuals of his day to keep their belief that matter was evil while pretending to follow Yeshua.

But in doing so, he stripped the gospel of its heart. The beauty of the incarnation, that Yehovah Himself entered His creation to redeem it, was replaced with an abstract story about a lesser god and a temporary spirit.

Paul warned of this long before Cerinthus appeared: "Don't let anyone capture you with empty philosophies and high-sounding nonsense that come from human thinking and from the spiritual powers of this world, rather than from Christ" (Colossians 2:8, NLT).

Cerinthus captured people with philosophy but emptied them of truth.

The Counter Gospel in Modern Form

Cerinthus' teaching lives on today in a different disguise. Whenever someone says, "The God of the Old Testament is angry and cruel, but Jesus is kind and loving," they echo Cerinthus.
Whenever pastors separate "the Jewish God" from "the Christian God," they echo Cerinthus.

Yeshua never came to reveal a new God. He came to show the world who Yehovah has always been.
He said, "If you had really known me, you would know who my Father is. From now on, you do know him and have seen him!" (John 14:7, NLT).

That statement destroys Cerinthus' entire system in one sentence.

Tracing Cerinthus' Influence

Cerinthus does not appear often in modern sermons, but his fingerprints are all over the deceptions that still trouble the Church today. He lived in the late first century, overlapping with the apostle John, and early writers record that John wrote his Gospel and letters with Cerinthus' teachings directly in view.

Cerinthus taught that Yeshua was only a human being and that the divine "Christ spirit" came upon Him at His baptism and left before the crucifixion. He separated the man from the Messiah. This was the beginning of what we now call adoptionism and separation Christology, ideas that would later flourish in full Gnosticism.

John confronted this deception with absolute clarity.

1 John 4:2 to 3 (NLT):
"If a person claiming to be a prophet acknowledges that Yeshua the Messiah came in a real body, that person has the Spirit of God. But if someone claims that Yeshua did not come in the flesh, that person is not from God."

Cerinthus used Scripture, spoke like a believer, and claimed to honor Yeshua. That is why so many were confused. But every lie he taught rested on one great denial. He denied that Yeshua is Yehovah in the flesh.

How Cerinthus' Ideas Survived

Even after Cerinthus died, his teachings continued to flow into other movements.

They influenced:

- the Gnostic division between the man Jesus and the heavenly Christ
- the claim that the divine could not suffer, so only the human part of Jesus died
- the idea that revelation comes through mystical knowledge instead of the written Word

- the belief that obedience is optional because salvation is found in inner spiritual enlightenment

These seeds later shaped the systems of Valentinus, Basilides, and many Gnostic groups throughout the Roman Empire.

Cerinthus in Today's Church

His influence did not disappear. It simply changed forms.

Modern versions include ideas such as:

- "Jesus was a great teacher, but not fully divine."
- Treating Yeshua as less than the Father instead of one with Him.
- Claiming Yeshua set aside His divinity during His earthly life.
- Dividing the historical Jesus from the Christ of faith.
- Teaching that obedience is optional because only spiritual things matter.

These ideas are heard in seminaries, pulpits, and popular books. Some are spoken openly. Others are quietly assumed. Cerinthus would feel at home in many churches today.

Why This Matters Now

If Yeshua is not Yehovah in the flesh, then the entire Gospel collapses.

- His sacrifice cannot save us.
- His resurrection loses its power.
- His teachings lose their authority.
- His identity becomes negotiable.

Cerinthus attacked the foundation. John responded by calling this teaching the spirit of antichrist. He did not use that word lightly. He used it for a direct denial of Yeshua's divine identity.

The Answer Today Is the Same

We confront Cerinthus the same way the apostle John did.

- We hold fast to the truth that Yeshua is Yehovah made flesh.
- We reject every teaching that separates the man from the Messiah.
- We stay rooted in Scripture, not mystical claims or special revelation.
- We walk in the commandments, because truth and obedience belong together.

History teaches a simple lesson. What the Church fails to confront eventually takes root. What we refuse to discern will shape us.

Cerinthus is long gone, but his teachings still whisper through modern theology. It falls to the faithful remnant to answer those whispers with truth, clarity, and loyalty to who Yeshua truly is.

The heresy of Cerinthus is more than history. It is a mirror. It shows how easily people trade revelation for reason, or the living God of Scripture for a philosophical idea that feels safer.

The same spirit that tried to divide Yeshua from Yehovah still whispers today: "You can believe in Jesus without all that Old Testament stuff." But Yeshua is the very Word that gave the Old Testament life.

John's Gospel, the writings of Paul, and the witness of the early Church all stand on one unshakable truth: the Creator of Genesis

THE RISE OF MARCION AND THE FALL OF THE FAITHFUL

and the Redeemer of Calvary are one and the same, Yehovah revealed in Yeshua.

Reflection Questions

1. Why did Cerinthus believe the God of the Old Testament was inferior, and how does that view affect faith today?
2. How does John's Gospel directly refute Cerinthus' theology about creation and the incarnation?
3. Why is it important to affirm that Yeshua and Yehovah are one, not separate deities?

Key Scriptures (NLT)

- John 1:1–14
- 1 John 2:18–23
- Colossians 2:8–9
- John 14:7–9
- Deuteronomy 6:4

Primary Sources for Footnotes

1. Eusebius, *Ecclesiastical History*, 3.28, quoting Irenaeus, in *Nicene and Post-Nicene Fathers*, Vol. 1 (Grand Rapids: Eerdmans, 1955).

2. Irenaeus, *Against Heresies*, 1.26.1, in *Ante-Nicene Fathers*, Vol. 1 (Edinburgh: T&T Clark, 1885).

3. Epiphanius, *Panarion*, 28.1–2, in *Nicene and Post-Nicene Fathers*, Series 2, Vol. 6 (Grand Rapids: Eerdmans, 1899).

4. Ibid., 28.6–7.

5. Irenaeus, *Against Heresies*, 1.26.1.

6. Eusebius, *Ecclesiastical History*, 3.28.

7. Hippolytus, *Refutation of All Heresies*, 7.33, in *Ante-Nicene Fathers*, Vol. 5 (Edinburgh: T&T Clark, 1886).

8. Epiphanius, *Panarion*, 28.7.

Chapter 5 Valentinus and the System of Secret Knowledge

The Allure of the Hidden

If Simon Magus represented power without purity, Nicolas represented grace without law, and Cerinthus represented philosophy without revelation, then Valentinus represents religion without relationship.

He took the scattered ideas of these earlier heretics and built them into an impressive structure that looked spiritual on the outside but hollowed out the faith from within.
From Simon he inherited the hunger for power.
From Nicolas he borrowed the comfort of compromise.
From Cerinthus he adopted the separation between the Creator and the Redeemer.

By the middle of the second century, Valentinus was the most influential teacher in Rome. He was eloquent, educated, and persuasive. He talked about Yeshua, salvation, and even grace, but behind those words he built a new system based not on Scripture but on secret knowledge.

People loved it because it made them feel special.

A Man of Influence

Valentinus was born in Egypt around AD 100 and educated in Alexandria, the same intellectual center that shaped Cerinthus a

THE RISE OF MARCION AND THE FALL OF THE FAITHFUL

generation earlier.[1] He studied both Jewish allegory and Greek philosophy, blending them with Christian vocabulary.

When he moved to Rome around AD 135, he quickly rose to prominence. According to Tertullian, Valentinus nearly became bishop of Rome before his teachings were exposed as false.[2] His charisma drew crowds, but his gospel was a clever counterfeit.

What We Really Know About Valentinus

Early writers like Irenaeus, Tertullian, and Hippolytus preserved detailed accounts of his beliefs.

1. He taught that God is an unknowable, invisible source called the Depth. From this Depth came thirty lesser beings called *aeons,* forming a divine hierarchy known as the *Pleroma.*[3]

2. He claimed the material world was created by a lesser, fallen being named Sophia (Wisdom). Her error gave birth to the Creator of the physical world, the same false god Cerinthus called the demiurge.[4]

3. He reinterpreted salvation as a return to secret knowledge. In his view, Yeshua came not to die for sin but to awaken divine knowledge within select souls.[5]

4. He divided humanity into three classes. The *spiritual* (who could receive the hidden truth), the *soulish* (ordinary believers), and the *material* (those beyond saving).[6]

5. He used Scripture symbolically rather than historically. He claimed every story in the Bible was a coded message revealing cosmic mysteries known only to the enlightened.[7]

THE RISE OF MARCION AND THE FALL OF THE FAITHFUL

Valentinus took the fragments of Gnostic thought from Alexandria and turned them into a complete theology. To many, it looked sophisticated, but it completely denied the simplicity of the gospel.

The Lure of Gnostic Superiority

The attraction of Valentinus' message was pride. He told people they could be part of a secret inner circle that possessed revelation hidden from the average believer.

That mindset directly contradicts Yeshua's words:

"You are permitted to understand the secrets of the Kingdom of Heaven, but others are not" (Matthew 13:11, NLT).

Yeshua revealed truth to His followers freely, not through secret initiation. But Valentinus claimed that salvation depended on mystical insight rather than repentance and faith.

Gnosticism always starts with the same promise, that you can have wisdom apart from obedience. It is the same lie the serpent told Eve, "You will be like God, knowing both good and evil" (Genesis 3:5, NLT).

How Valentinus Viewed Yehovah

Like Cerinthus, Valentinus saw the God of the Old Testament as a lesser, ignorant being. He taught that this Creator, often called the demiurge, was proud and jealous, unaware of the higher spiritual realm above Him.[8]
He argued that the Law of Moses came from this lower being and

THE RISE OF MARCION AND THE FALL OF THE FAITHFUL

therefore needed to be transcended through knowledge, not obeyed in faith.

In this system, Yehovah was not the Father of Yeshua but a cosmic obstacle.
This view completely inverted the truth. Yeshua Himself said, "I and the Father are one" (John 10:30, NLT).

Valentinus' theology replaced covenant with complexity. He took the living God of Abraham and turned Him into a metaphor.

John's Warning Comes to Life

John's earlier warnings about the "spirit of antichrist" (1 John 4:3, NLT) were coming true in Valentinus' time. The same false separation between the Creator and the Redeemer had evolved into a sophisticated belief system.

Irenaeus wrote, "By transferring what is said of the true God to the invented being of their own imagination, they act as if they had already surpassed the apostles."[9]
That single statement captures Gnosticism's heart. It always believes it knows more than the apostles, more than the prophets, and ultimately more than Yehovah Himself.

A Gospel Without Grace

In Valentinus' view, Yeshua did not come to shed His blood for sin. He came as a messenger from the Pleroma to remind divine souls of their forgotten origin. Salvation was not through faith or forgiveness but through enlightenment.

That idea contradicts the entire message of Scripture. Paul wrote, "God saved you by his grace when you believed. And you can't take credit for this; it is a gift from God" (Ephesians 2:8, NLT).

Valentinus' religion appealed to intellect but denied grace. It replaced the humility of the cross with the pride of knowledge.

The true gospel says, "Anyone who comes to God must believe that he exists and that he rewards those who sincerely seek him" (Hebrews 11:6, NLT). Gnosticism says, "You can find your own way if you know enough."

The difference is eternal.

The Legacy of Valentinus

Valentinus trained disciples who spread his ideas throughout the Roman Empire. Even after his death around AD 160, his followers divided into branches such as the *Eastern Valentinians* and *Western Valentinians*.
Their writings blended Scripture with philosophy so effectively that many Christians confused them for legitimate teachers.

Clement of Alexandria even quoted Valentinian ideas sympathetically before later rejecting them.[10]
By the third century, these ideas had become so widespread that nearly every church council had to confront them.

Valentinus' system shaped later heresies like the teachings of Basilides, the *Gospel of Truth,* and even portions of the Nag Hammadi texts discovered in modern times. His name became synonymous with secret knowledge that replaces the simplicity of the cross.

THE RISE OF MARCION AND THE FALL OF THE FAITHFUL

Tracing Valentinus' Influence

You can still hear Valentinus today. He speaks every time someone says, "I have a higher revelation that most Christians don't understand."

He whispers in movements that promise hidden mysteries or inner awakenings that go beyond Scripture.

But Paul said clearly, "Christ makes us complete. So you also are complete through your union with Christ, who is the head over every ruler and authority" (Colossians 2:10, NLT).
There is no secret level beyond that.

The moment someone tells you they have discovered something "the Church has hidden," you can be sure they are walking in Valentinus' footsteps.

Why This Matters Now

Valentinus built a religion that looked holy but removed the need for repentance, faith, and humility. His system replaced dependence on the Holy Spirit with dependence on intellect.

The Church today still faces the same temptation, to turn faith into formulas, theology into theory, and revelation into riddles.

But the Kingdom of God was never meant to be a puzzle. It was meant to be a relationship.
Yeshua said, "Unless you turn from your sins and become like little children, you will never get into the Kingdom of Heaven" (Matthew 18:3, NLT).

THE RISE OF MARCION AND THE FALL OF THE FAITHFUL

The gospel is not about how much you know. It is about who you know, and whether your heart belongs to Him.

And though Valentinus' followers called themselves the enlightened, his theology of elitism would echo for centuries. In time, the same ideas about divine selection, hidden revelation, and spiritual hierarchy would resurface under new names and polished theology, a topic we will revisit in the second section of this book.

Reflection Questions

1. Why was Valentinus' message so appealing to the intellectual culture of Rome and Alexandria?
2. How does the idea of secret revelation still tempt believers today?
3. Why is simplicity in the gospel a mark of truth, not weakness?

Key Scriptures (NLT)

- Matthew 13:11
- Genesis 3:5
- John 10:30
- Colossians 2:8–10
- Ephesians 2:8–9
- Matthew 18:3

Primary Sources for Footnotes

1. Eusebius, *Ecclesiastical History*, 4.11, in *Nicene and Post-Nicene Fathers*, Vol. 1 (Grand Rapids: Eerdmans, 1955).

2. Tertullian, *Against the Valentinians*, 4, in *Ante-Nicene Fathers*, Vol. 3 (Edinburgh: T&T Clark, 1885).

3. Irenaeus, *Against Heresies*, 1.1–1.2, in *Ante-Nicene Fathers*, Vol. 1 (Edinburgh: T&T Clark, 1885).

4. Hippolytus, *Refutation of All Heresies*, 6.30, in *Ante-Nicene Fathers*, Vol. 5 (Edinburgh: T&T Clark, 1886).

5. Irenaeus, *Against Heresies*, 1.6.1.

6. Ibid., 1.7.5.

7. Hippolytus, *Refutation of All Heresies*, 6.34.

8. Irenaeus, *Against Heresies*, 1.5.4.

9. Ibid., 1.9.4.

10. Clement of Alexandria, *Stromata*, 2.8, in *Ante-Nicene Fathers*, Vol. 2 (Edinburgh: T&T Clark, 1885).

THE RISE OF MARCION AND THE FALL OF THE FAITHFUL

Chapter 6 Marcion and the Great Divide

When the God of the Bible Became the Enemy

If Simon Magus chased power, Nicolas abused grace, Cerinthus corrupted truth, and Valentinus intellectualized faith, then Marcion went further than them all. He did not simply distort the gospel; he tried to divide it.

Marcion drew a line through the Bible itself, separating what he called the "God of wrath" in the Old Testament from the "God of love" revealed in Yeshua. He claimed they were two different beings, two separate deities, locked in moral conflict.

It was the most dangerous idea the early Church had ever faced because it sounded compassionate. Marcion's teaching was not born in hatred but in misunderstanding. He thought he was rescuing Christianity from the God of judgment, but in doing so, he created a new religion entirely.

A Wealthy Man with a Wounded Faith

Marcion was born around AD 85 in Sinope, a port city on the southern coast of the Black Sea. His father was reportedly a bishop, and Marcion grew up surrounded by the Church.[1] He became a successful shipowner, wealthy and educated, and eventually moved to Rome around AD 135.

At first, he tried to join the Church there. He even gave the Roman congregation a large donation, a gift of 200,000 sesterces, roughly equivalent to seven million dollars today. But when his teachings

THE RISE OF MARCION AND THE FALL OF THE FAITHFUL

were found to contradict the apostles' writings, he was excommunicated, and his money returned.

That rejection did not humble him. It hardened him. Marcion left the Church convinced that he, not the bishops, understood the true gospel.

What We Really Know About Marcion

The early fathers wrote more about Marcion than nearly any other heretic. From their writings, especially Irenaeus and Tertullian, we can outline his key beliefs.

1. He rejected the Old Testament entirely. Marcion claimed the Creator God of Israel was not the Father of Yeshua but a lower, cruel deity obsessed with law and punishment.[3]

2. He created his own canon of Scripture. Marcion was the first to assemble a "New Testament," but his version was deeply edited. He accepted only one Gospel and ten of Paul's letters, removing or rewriting anything that connected Yeshua to the Hebrew Scriptures or to the Creator.[4]

    - Gospel: a shortened and edited version of *Luke*, which he called *The Gospel of the Lord*. He removed the first two chapters describing Yeshua's birth, every Old Testament quotation, and any mention of prophecy or fulfillment. The Gospel began abruptly with Yeshua's appearance in Capernaum.
    - Paul's Letters (10 total):
        1. Galatians
        2. 1 Corinthians

3. 2 Corinthians
4. Romans
5. 1 Thessalonians
6. 2 Thessalonians
7. Laodiceans (Marcion's version of *Ephesians*, altered and renamed)
8. Colossians
9. Philippians
10. Philemon

- Even in these, Marcion made heavy edits. He deleted all Old Testament references, softened language about judgment, and removed words that tied Yeshua to Israel or Abraham's covenant.[5]

He rejected *1 and 2 Timothy* and *Titus*, calling them "too Jewish." He also removed *Hebrews* and anything written by Peter, James, or John. To him, the other apostles misunderstood Yeshua's mission because they were still loyal to the "Creator God."

3. He taught that Yeshua came from an unknown, higher God. According to Marcion, Yeshua appeared suddenly in human form but was not born of a woman. He came to deliver humanity from the Creator's tyranny.[6]

4. He denied the resurrection of the body. Like the Gnostics before him, Marcion viewed the physical world as evil and unworthy of redemption.[7]

THE RISE OF MARCION AND THE FALL OF THE FAITHFUL

5. He built a rival church system. Marcion established his own bishops, congregations, and missionaries, spreading his theology across the Roman Empire for nearly three centuries.[8]

In essence, Marcion took Cerinthus' view of a flawed Creator and Valentinus' idea of a higher, hidden God and combined them into a single, organized movement. He gave Gnosticism a pulpit and a budget.

How Marcion Viewed Yehovah

To Marcion, Yehovah was a god of justice without mercy, a ruler who demanded obedience through fear. He read the Old Testament without understanding its purpose. Every act of judgment appeared cruel, every law oppressive, every punishment excessive.

He saw no continuity between the God of Abraham and the Father of Yeshua. He taught that the Creator's harsh commands in the Torah proved that He was not good, and that Yeshua's grace revealed an entirely new God, one of love, forgiveness, and acceptance.[8]

But Marcion's error was not seeing the whole story. He missed that the same God who said, "I have set before you life and death, blessings and curses" (Deuteronomy 30:19, NLT) is also the one who said, "I have loved you with an everlasting love" (Jeremiah 31:3, NLT).

The God of the Old Testament is the God of grace who gave second chances again and again. He clothed Adam and Eve. He spared Noah. He chose Abraham. He delivered Israel. He forgave David.

THE RISE OF MARCION AND THE FALL OF THE FAITHFUL

And He promised a Redeemer long before the cross ever appeared on Calvary.

Marcion could not reconcile judgment and mercy in one God. But the Bible never separated them.

Paul's Gospel and Marcion's Twist

Marcion called himself a follower of Paul, yet he mutilated Paul's writings to fit his system.

He loved Paul's words about grace but ignored his warnings about sin. He quoted Ephesians 2:8–9 but rejected Romans 3:31, where Paul wrote, "Well then, if we emphasize faith, does this mean that we can forget about the law? Of course not! In fact, only when we have faith do we truly fulfill the law" (NLT).

Marcion wanted Paul without Moses, grace without covenant, faith without obedience.

Paul, however, taught that the Torah was holy, just, and good (Romans 7:12). He saw it as the revelation of God's character, not the invention of a cruel deity. Marcion removed the Hebrew roots of the gospel and left a faith floating in air, disconnected from its foundation.

THE RISE OF MARCION AND THE FALL OF THE FAITHFUL

The Great Divide

Marcion's movement created a permanent rift. He was the first to publish a "New Testament" in history, but his version excluded most of it. He drew a sharp line between Judaism and Christianity, rejecting everything that tied Yeshua to Israel.

That division still shapes much of the Western Church today. When believers say, "We're not under the Old Testament anymore," they echo Marcion's language, not Paul's.

Paul never abolished the Scriptures; he fulfilled them in Messiah. Yeshua said, "Don't misunderstand why I have come. I did not come to abolish the law of Moses or the writings of the prophets. No, I came to accomplish their purpose" (Matthew 5:17, NLT).

Marcion built his theology on misunderstanding that one truth.

Why the Early Church Fought So Hard

The early fathers understood that Marcion's gospel would destroy Christianity if left unchallenged. Irenaeus wrote entire volumes against him, showing that the same God who sent the prophets sent the Son.[9]

Tertullian called Marcion "the Pontic wolf" because he devoured entire churches with his doctrines.[10] Yet even in opposing him, the Church learned to define the canon of Scripture more clearly. God used Marcion's rebellion to push the Church toward unity and clarity.

Without Marcion, we might not have the same confidence in the New Testament today. His attempt to edit the Bible forced believers to protect it.

THE RISE OF MARCION AND THE FALL OF THE FAITHFUL

A New Gospel for a New Age

Marcion's appeal was emotional. He wanted a faith of love without law, mercy without judgment, and forgiveness without repentance. He made the gospel comfortable.

His followers were sincere, moral, and disciplined, but their devotion was built on a lie. They worshiped a God who did not exist and followed a Savior who never became flesh.

This new gospel still sounds appealing today. Many churches, in trying to avoid sounding harsh or judgmental, have drifted toward Marcion's view without realizing it. They teach that God's love cancels His standards, that grace means freedom from obedience, and that sin no longer needs repentance.

But the true gospel does not remove the law. It writes it on our hearts.
"This is the new covenant I will make with the people of Israel on that day," says the Lord. "I will put my instructions deep within them, and I will write them on their hearts. I will be their God, and they will be my people" (Jeremiah 31:33, NLT).

Yehovah's law and Yeshua's grace were never enemies. They have always been one voice of the same God.

Tracing Marcion's Influence

The spirit of Marcion is alive in modern theology. It appears whenever someone says, "That's just the Old Testament," as though the first two-thirds of the Bible no longer matter. It thrives in teachings that separate Yeshua from His Jewish identity or remove the need for obedience to His commands.

It even echoes in movements that overemphasize grace while rejecting God's expectations.
Some theologians, knowingly or not, have reintroduced Marcion's worldview in a refined form, dividing law and grace, Israel and the Church, Old Testament and New.

In the second section of this book, we will explore how those ideas resurfaced centuries later in new systems of theology that shaped entire denominations. The same old error of Marcion still whispers through doctrines that pit God's justice against His mercy and His law against His love.

Why This Matters

Marcion is long dead, but his ideas are not. They have been baptized into Christian vocabulary, wrapped in modern language, and quietly woven into the beliefs of countless churches. Many believers who would never call themselves Marcionites still repeat his doctrine without realizing where it came from.

Any time we hear someone say...

"God was different in the Old Testament."
"Jesus replaced the Law with grace."
"Paul preached a new religion."
"Israel was set aside and the Church replaced her."
"The Old Testament is not for us today."

...we are hearing Marcion's voice echo through the centuries.

THE RISE OF MARCION AND THE FALL OF THE FAITHFUL

This matters because Marcion did not simply misunderstand a few verses. He attacked the very character of God. He tore the Bible in half. He rejected the Scriptures Yeshua loved, quoted, and fulfilled. And he created the first systematic attempt to separate believers from the foundation God Himself laid.

When the Church forgets its roots, it loses its identity.
When it rejects Torah, it loses its definition of sin.
When it separates Yeshua from Yehovah, it loses the Gospel itself.

Marcion's influence leads to a faith with no anchor. A Messiah with no covenant. A Gospel with no foundation. A grace with no holiness. It creates a Christianity that honors Jesus with the lips but denies the Scriptures He trusted with His life.

The early Church knew this danger. That is why they fought Marcion with such urgency. They understood what was at stake. They knew the Gospel could not survive if the Scriptures were divided and the God of Israel was rejected.

We face the same challenge today.
The names have changed, but the doctrine has not.
The language has softened, but the message is identical.

If we do not confront these ideas, they will continue to shape how people read the Bible, how they see Yeshua, and how they live out their faith.

The call of this chapter is simple.
Return to the apostles' faith.
Return to the Scriptures Yeshua cherished.
Return to the God who never changes.
Return to the unity of Law and grace, Word and Spirit, Israel and the nations ... brought together in the Messiah.

THE RISE OF MARCION AND THE FALL OF THE FAITHFUL

Marcion tried to rewrite the story.
Yeshua invites us to return to the real one.

Reflection Questions

1. Why did Marcion see the Old Testament as incompatible with Yeshua's message?

2. How does Marcion's edited version of Scripture compare to modern interpretations that downplay the Hebrew roots of faith?

3. Why is it important to see both judgment and mercy as part of Yehovah's character?

Key Scriptures (NLT)

- Matthew 5:17
- Romans 7:12
- Jeremiah 31:33
- Deuteronomy 30:19
- Jeremiah 31:3
- Ephesians 2:8–9
- Romans 3:31

THE RISE OF MARCION AND THE FALL OF THE FAITHFUL

Primary Sources for Footnotes

1. Tertullian, *Against Marcion*, 1.1, in *Ante-Nicene Fathers*, Vol. 3 (Edinburgh: T&T Clark, 1885).

2. Ibid., 4.4.

3. Irenaeus, *Against Heresies*, 1.27.4, in *Ante-Nicene Fathers*, Vol. 1 (Edinburgh: T&T Clark, 1885).

4. Tertullian, *Against Marcion*, 4.2.

5. Ibid., 4.8.

6. Irenaeus, *Against Heresies*, 1.27.3.

7. Eusebius, *Ecclesiastical History*, 4.11.

8. Epiphanius, *Panarion*, 42.1–4.

9. Irenaeus, *Against Heresies*, 3.12.12.

10. Tertullian, *Against Marcion*, 1.14.

THE RISE OF MARCION AND THE FALL OF THE FAITHFUL

Part 2 Heresies Revived

False teaching never stays buried. What once threatened the early believers has resurfaced in new forms, new language, and new packaging. The enemy rarely invents fresh lies; he simply recycles the old ones. The same distortions that troubled the first-century Church are alive and well in our own generation.

Part 2 reveals how those ancient heresies reappear today. You will recognize the same patterns - rejecting Torah, dividing the Scriptures, elevating knowledge over obedience, and separating Yeshua from His own identity as the God of Israel. Modern Christianity has unknowingly revived ideas the early fathers condemned.

This section will show you:

- How Gnosticism now hides in modern spirituality
- How Marcion's views appear in teachings that remove the Old Testament
- How lawlessness is normalized by twisting Paul's words
- How the Church adopted ideas the apostles never taught
- How identity, covenant, and holiness were redefined by culture

And through it all, you will see one truth: when the foundations are neglected, deception always returns.

Part 2 will help you see how ancient errors return when the foundations are ignored.

Chapter 7 The Heresy That Never Died

Old Lies in New Language

When Marcion died around AD 160, his followers continued to grow in number. The early Church thought his heresy would fade with time, but it did not. It simply changed its clothes.

Marcion's ideas never disappeared; they resurfaced century after century under new names and refined language. Every time someone divided the Bible into "Old Testament God" versus "New Testament Jesus," Marcion lived again.

His movement lasted for more than 300 years, long after his death. Even when the Church officially condemned his teachings, his influence kept spreading quietly through philosophy, theology, and interpretation. The face changed, but the core remained the same, a refusal to see the oneness of Yehovah and Yeshua.

The Same Spirit in Different Centuries

Marcion's theology became a seedbed for several later distortions of the faith. While these systems often disagreed on the details, they shared his central error: dividing law and grace, justice and mercy, or Israel and the Church.

1. Replacement Theology (also called Supersessionism) argued that the Church had replaced Israel as God's people. This view quietly removed Israel's covenant identity and treated the Hebrew Scriptures as background history instead of ongoing revelation.

- The New Testament never teaches this. Paul wrote, "Did God reject his own people, the nation of Israel? Of course not!" (Romans 11:1, NLT).
- Yet Marcion's old idea (that the God of Israel was finished) became the foundation for centuries of theology that ignored the promises of the Tanakh.

2. Dispensationalism eventually arose in the 1800s as a reaction, but it still carried traces of Marcion's split. It divided God's dealings into separate eras and sometimes suggested that the Old Testament law no longer applied to believers at all.
   - It emphasized grace but often detached it from the continuity of Torah.
   - Marcion would have agreed with the separation but for the opposite reason; he rejected the law because he thought it was evil, while dispensationalists rejected it because they thought it was obsolete.

3. Calvinism carried echoes of Valentinus and Marcion in its rigid structure of divine selection and limited salvation. While it was not intentionally heretical, its framework reintroduced a sense of spiritual hierarchy ... the chosen and the unchosen, the elect and the reprobate ... that resembled the elitism of Gnosticism.
   - Calvin's system, shaped in the 1500s, was intellectually brilliant and sincere, but it mirrored the old tendency to confine grace to a limited group.

THE RISE OF MARCION AND THE FALL OF THE FAITHFUL

- In practice, this made the gospel sound less like "whosoever believes" (John 3:16, NLT) and more like "whoever has already been chosen."

These theologies, though different in form and motive, show how Marcion's influence seeped through Christian history. The names changed, but the division remained: grace against law, love against justice, and Church against Israel.

The Appeal of Division

Marcion's ideas thrive because they make faith easier.
It feels simpler to separate the "God of wrath" from the "God of love" than to accept that both are one. It feels safer to say the Old Testament no longer matters than to wrestle with what it truly means.

Modern believers often carry this split without realizing it. Phrases like "That was the Old Testament" or "We're under grace, not law" echo Marcion's theology, not Yeshua's.

Yeshua said, "Anyone who listens to my teaching and follows it is wise, like a person who builds a house on solid rock" (Matthew 7:24, NLT). He never dismissed His Father's commands; He fulfilled them and taught others to do the same.

The Church loses power whenever it separates what God has joined together.

THE RISE OF MARCION AND THE FALL OF THE FAITHFUL

How the Lie Survived

Marcion's teaching survived because it appealed to two human desires: comfort and control.

- Comfort: By removing the God of judgment, Marcion made people feel safe without repentance.
- Control: By rejecting the Hebrew Scriptures, he freed teachers from accountability to God's standard.

Centuries later, those same motives appear in modern theology. Some emphasize love so much that holiness disappears. Others treat God's law as outdated, claiming that "relationship" makes obedience unnecessary.

But true relationship produces obedience. Yeshua said, "If you love me, obey my commandments" (John 14:15, NLT).

When love rejects obedience, it ceases to be love.

The Cost of Forgetting Our Roots

When the Church lost connection to the Hebrew roots of faith, it lost context for Yeshua's mission.
The festivals, the priesthood, the sacrifices, and the Torah were not relics of a failed religion. They were shadows pointing to Him.

Marcion threw away the shadow and misunderstood the substance. Modern Christianity often repeats the mistake by rejecting everything "Jewish" as irrelevant. Yet Paul warned against this arrogance:

"You Gentiles were branches from a wild olive tree, and you were grafted in. So do not boast about being grafted in to replace the branches that were broken off. Remember, you are not supporting the root; the root is supporting you" (Romans 11:17–18, NLT).

Whenever the Church forgets its root, it loses its fruit.

A Return to the Whole Gospel

The solution to Marcion's heresy is not to swing back into legalism but to rediscover the wholeness of Scripture. The same Spirit who inspired Moses inspired Paul. The same Yehovah who thundered at Sinai hung on a cross at Golgotha.

Law and grace are not rivals. Law reveals our need for grace, and grace empowers us to live out the law from the heart.

Paul said, "For God's will was for us to be made holy by the sacrifice of the body of Jesus Christ, once for all time" (Hebrews 10:10, NLT).
Holiness was never abolished; it was fulfilled in us through the Spirit.

The early Church fought to preserve this truth. Our generation must fight to recover it.

Why This Matters Now

We live in an age where theology has become fragmented. People claim to follow Jesus but redefine His teachings to fit their preferences. The same subtle voice that whispered to Marcion still speaks today: "You can have Jesus without the law, faith without repentance, love without truth."

THE RISE OF MARCION AND THE FALL OF THE FAITHFUL

But Yeshua never offered that kind of discipleship.
He said, "If any of you wants to be my follower, you must give up your own way, take up your cross daily, and follow me" (Luke 9:23, NLT).

Truth always costs something. The only gospel that saves is the one that unites the Father's justice with the Son's mercy. Anything less is a partial gospel, and a partial gospel cannot save.

Reflection Questions

1. How have Marcion's ideas survived in modern theology, even among sincere believers?

2. Why is it dangerous to separate the Old Testament from the New Testament?

3. What does it mean to live under grace without rejecting God's law?

Key Scriptures (NLT)

- Romans 11:1
- Romans 11:17–18
- Matthew 5:17
- John 14:15
- Luke 9:23
- Matthew 7:24
- Hebrews 10:10

Primary Sources for Footnotes

1. Irenaeus, *Against Heresies*, 3.12.12, in *Ante-Nicene Fathers*, Vol. 1 (Edinburgh: T&T Clark, 1885).

2. Tertullian, *Against Marcion*, 4.2, in *Ante-Nicene Fathers*, Vol. 3 (Edinburgh: T&T Clark, 1885).

3. Eusebius, *Ecclesiastical History*, 4.11.

4. Justin Martyr, *First Apology*, 26.

5. Augustine, *Contra Faustum Manichaeum*, 15.7.

THE RISE OF MARCION AND THE FALL OF THE FAITHFUL

Chapter 8 Gnosticism in the Pulpit

When Knowledge Becomes a Stage

There is a growing problem in many churches today. It sounds spiritual. It even looks holy. But it is quietly dividing the Body of Messiah.

It begins when certain voices say, "We have deeper revelation." They speak as if some believers are "in the know" while others are still in the dark. These teachers are often charismatic, gifted, and persuasive. They promise access to secret wisdom or higher spiritual levels.

That mindset is not new. It is exactly what Valentinus taught in the second century. He was a master of charisma, eloquent and educated, and he convinced many that he alone could reveal hidden truths about God. His followers called themselves the "spiritual," while everyone else was "soulish" or "earthly."

The Church had seen Simon Magus chase power and Nicolas twist grace. With Valentinus, the danger was more subtle. He turned revelation into a performance.

The Church's Ancient Warning

The apostle Paul warned about this spirit in *Colossians 2:18–19 (NLT)*:

"Don't let anyone condemn you by insisting on pious self-denial or the worship of angels, saying they have had visions about these things. Their sinful minds have made them proud, and they are not connected to Christ, the head of the body."

Paul was confronting the same elitist attitude. Certain believers claimed special visions that made them spiritually superior. But Paul said their pride proved they were no longer connected to Messiah.

Knowledge that separates us from others is not revelation from God. True revelation always leads us back to humility and love.

Valentinus and the Birth of Religious Elitism

Valentinus lived in Alexandria, Egypt, the home of Gnosticism. His teachings blended Greek philosophy with biblical imagery. He spoke about a distant, unknowable God who could only be reached through secret understanding.

To him, not everyone was capable of salvation. Humanity was divided into three types:

1. The spiritual, who could be saved through hidden knowledge.
2. The soulish, who might be saved by faith and works.
3. The material, who were beyond redemption.

This created a spiritual class system that contradicted the gospel of Yeshua, who said, "Come to me, all of you who are weary and carry heavy burdens, and I will give you rest" (*Matthew 11:28, NLT*).

The message of Yeshua is open to everyone. The message of Valentinus was only for the few.

THE RISE OF MARCION AND THE FALL OF THE FAITHFUL

When the Pulpit Becomes a Platform

The same spirit of elitism has crept back into many modern pulpits. It appears when pastors and prophets claim revelation that cannot be questioned. It thrives when leaders act as though their private insight outweighs Scripture itself.

Whenever a teacher says, "You need me to interpret this for you," beware. That is how control begins. The apostles never claimed secret authority over the truth. They pointed people back to Scripture.

Irenaeus, the bishop of Lyons, wrote in *Against Heresies 3.2*:

"We have learned from none others the plan of our salvation, than from those through whom the Gospel has come down to us, which they did at one time proclaim in public, and, at a later period, by the will of God, handed down to us in the Scriptures."

He reminded the Church that revelation is not private property. It is written for all believers. The Scriptures belong to the whole Body, not just the few who claim special knowledge.

Why This Still Matters

Modern Gnosticism does not always call itself by that name. It hides behind terms like "prophetic secrets," "hidden codes," or "mysteries of the kingdom." It appeals to curiosity and pride, convincing people that truth can only be found through the teacher, not through the Word.

THE RISE OF MARCION AND THE FALL OF THE FAITHFUL

Yeshua never hid the path to salvation. He said, "I have spoken openly to the world. I have always taught in synagogues and in the temple, where everyone gathers" (*John 18:20, NLT*).

Any message that divides believers into insiders and outsiders is not the gospel. The Holy Spirit does not create cliques. He creates community.

When a church prizes revelation over Scripture, it repeats Valentinus' mistake. When a congregation begins to see its teacher as the only source of truth, it repeats his heresy.

Guarding the Faith

Hippolytus of Rome wrote his *Refutation of All Heresies* to expose this very problem. In his introduction, he said that false teachers "disguise themselves with the language of truth" to deceive the simple. His goal was not to mock them but to protect the Church from error.

Every generation has needed that protection. Our call is to test every spirit, compare every teaching with the Word, and stay rooted in the simplicity of Messiah.

Paul said, "Don't let anyone lead you astray with empty philosophies and high-sounding nonsense that come from human thinking and from the spiritual powers of this world, rather than from Christ" (*Colossians 2:8, NLT*).

Truth does not need to be dressed up. The gospel is powerful in its plainness.

THE RISE OF MARCION AND THE FALL OF THE FAITHFUL

The True Measure of Maturity

Spiritual maturity is not measured by how many mysteries we know but by how much we resemble Yeshua.

Peter said, "You must grow in the grace and knowledge of our Lord and Savior Jesus Christ" (*2 Peter 3:18, NLT*). Grace comes first. Knowledge follows. Without grace, knowledge becomes pride.

A healthy church teaches from Scripture, listens for the Spirit, and submits revelation to the Word. That kind of humility keeps the community safe and the gospel pure.

Reflection Questions

1. How can you tell the difference between true revelation and spiritual elitism?
2. Why is it dangerous to build a ministry on private visions or secret insights?
3. What does it look like to stay humble in your pursuit of spiritual understanding?

Key Scriptures (NLT)

- Colossians 2:8
- Colossians 2:18–19
- Matthew 11:28
- John 18:20
- 2 Peter 3:18

THE RISE OF MARCION AND THE FALL OF THE FAITHFUL

Primary Sources for Footnotes

1. Irenaeus, *Against Heresies* 3.2, in *Ante-Nicene Fathers*, Vol. 1 (Edinburgh: T&T Clark, 1885).

2. Hippolytus, *Refutation of All Heresies*, Introduction (public domain).

THE RISE OF MARCION AND THE FALL OF THE FAITHFUL

Chapter 9 Grace Without Holiness

The Lie That Grace Cancels Obedience

If Gnosticism corrupted truth through pride, the Nicolaitans corrupted grace through compromise.
They claimed to follow Yeshua but lived like the world. They treated holiness as optional and repentance as outdated.

Their teaching was not about knowledge like Valentinus but about license. They believed grace meant freedom from moral restraint. That same spirit still whispers in churches today, telling believers that obedience is legalism and that holiness is unnecessary.

Yeshua addressed this directly in His letters to the churches of Revelation. He said, "You have some Nicolaitans among you who follow the same teaching. Repent of your sin, or I will come to you suddenly and fight against them with the sword of my mouth" (*Revelation 2:15–16, NLT*).

Grace does not erase the need for obedience. It empowers it.

Who Were the Nicolaitans?

Nicolas was one of the seven deacons chosen in Acts 6 to serve the believers in Jerusalem. Early records suggest he began faithfully, but later compromised. Church fathers like Irenaeus and Hippolytus describe him as the founder of a group that mixed faith in Yeshua with pagan immorality.

THE RISE OF MARCION AND THE FALL OF THE FAITHFUL

One ancient source reports that Nicolas demonstrated his "liberty" by allowing others to sleep with his wife, claiming it proved he was free from jealousy.[1] That attitude summed up the Nicolaitan error: confusing liberty with lawlessness.

While the details are debated, the results were clear. His followers justified sexual immorality and idolatry, teaching that grace covered every indulgence. They forgot that grace was never meant to excuse sin but to overcome it.

Turning Grace into a License

Jude warned against this very distortion.

"I say this because some ungodly people have wormed their way into your churches, saying that God's marvelous grace allows us to live immoral lives. The condemnation of such people was recorded long ago, for they have denied our only Master and Lord, Jesus Christ" (*Jude 4, NLT*).

Grace is not a license to sin. It is the power to live differently.

Peter said the same thing:

"Because of his glory and excellence, he has given us great and precious promises. These are the promises that enable you to share his divine nature and escape the world's corruption caused by human desires" (*2 Peter 1:4, NLT*).

Holiness is not legalism. It is evidence that grace has done its work.

THE RISE OF MARCION AND THE FALL OF THE FAITHFUL

When the Church Repeats the Error

Many modern churches preach a message that sounds compassionate but leaves people in bondage. They say, "You are under grace, not law," yet forget what Paul actually meant.

Paul wrote, "Sin is no longer your master, for you no longer live under the requirements of the law. Instead, you live under the freedom of God's grace" (*Romans 6:14, NLT*). Then he asked the question everyone still needs to hear:

"Well then, since God's grace has set us free from the law, does that mean we can go on sinning? Of course not!" (*Romans 6:15, NLT*).

Grace frees us from sin, not from obedience.

When grace is preached without repentance, it creates a Christianity without transformation. People confess Yeshua with their lips but continue to live as if He never rose from the dead. That is not freedom. It is deception.

The Danger of Lawlessness

Yeshua said there would come a day when many who claimed to follow Him would stand before His throne, expecting approval, only to hear the most sobering words ever spoken:

"Not everyone who calls out to me, 'Lord, Lord!' will enter the Kingdom of Heaven. Only those who actually do the will of my Father in heaven will enter. On judgment day many will say to me, 'Lord, Lord, we prophesied in your name and cast out demons in your name and performed many miracles in your name.' But I will reply, 'I never knew you. Get away from me, you who break God's laws'" (*Matthew 7:21–23, NLT*).

THE RISE OF MARCION AND THE FALL OF THE FAITHFUL

The phrase "you who break God's laws" reveals that lawlessness, not weakness, separates people from Yeshua. Grace does not cancel law. It writes it on our hearts.

True Grace Produces Holiness

Grace is more than pardon. It is power. Paul said, "For the grace of God has been revealed, bringing salvation to all people. And we are instructed to turn from godless living and sinful pleasures. We should live in this evil world with wisdom, righteousness, and devotion to God" (*Titus 2:11–12, NLT*).

If grace does not lead to righteousness, it is not biblical grace.

Yehovah's goal has never changed. From Mount Sinai to Pentecost, His desire has been to dwell among a people who reflect His holiness. Grace did not erase that calling. It fulfilled it.

Why This Matters Now

The modern "hyper-grace" movement often begins with good intentions. It wants to lift the weight of legalism and show people God's love. But when it removes repentance and obedience, it creates spiritual apathy.

The Church becomes comfortable with sin instead of being convicted by it. The result is a generation that claims to love Yeshua but denies His authority.

James warned about this kind of faith:

"How foolish! Can't you see that faith without good deeds is useless?" (*James 2:20, NLT*).

THE RISE OF MARCION AND THE FALL OF THE FAITHFUL

True grace produces good works. It does not excuse bad ones.

A Return to Balance

The Torah is not the enemy. Lawlessness is.

Paul said, "The law itself is holy, and its commands are holy and right and good" (*Romans 7:12, NLT*). The problem is not the standard. The problem is sin within us. Grace does not remove the standard. It gives us the power to meet it.

He made this clear again in *Romans 3:31*:

"Well then, if we emphasize faith, does this mean that we can forget about the law? Of course not! In fact, only when we have faith do we truly fulfill the law" (*Romans 3:31, NLT*).

Paul's point could not be clearer. True faith does not destroy Torah; it establishes it.

John, writing decades after the resurrection, taught the same truth. He defined sin by the same measure God gave Israel at Sinai:

"Everyone who practices sin also practices lawlessness; indeed, sin is lawlessness" (*1 John 3:4, NLT*).

The Greek word translated *lawlessness* is ἀνομία (anomia), from *a-* meaning "without" and *nomos* meaning "law" or "Torah." Literally, *anomia* means "without Torah."

Every time the Greek Septuagint, the translation of the Hebrew Scriptures used in the first century, uses *nomos*, it refers to the Torah, God's instruction and teaching. So when John wrote that "sin is anomia," he was saying that sin is the violation of Torah.

THE RISE OF MARCION AND THE FALL OF THE FAITHFUL

This is crucial because John wrote his letters around AD 90, nearly sixty years after Yeshua rose from the dead. The same apostle who leaned on Yeshua's chest at the Last Supper still defined sin in relation to Torah. That means the standard of righteousness had not changed after the cross.

John was not preaching legalism. He was explaining that grace does not change what sin is. It changes our ability to overcome it.

Yeshua fulfilled the law not so we could ignore it, but so we could finally live it out from the heart.

Reflection Questions

1. What is the difference between true grace and false grace?
2. Why does grace always lead to obedience rather than away from it?
3. How can you personally guard against turning liberty into lawlessness?

Key Scriptures (NLT)

- Revelation 2:14–16
- Jude 3–4
- Romans 6:14–15
- Titus 2:11–12
- Matthew 7:21–23
- Romans 3:31

THE RISE OF MARCION AND THE FALL OF THE FAITHFUL

- 1 John 3:4
- Romans 7:12
- James 2:20

Primary Sources for Footnotes

1. Clement of Alexandria, *Stromata* 2.20, and Epiphanius, *Panarion* 25.2 (public domain references to Nicolas and his followers).

Chapter 10 Cerinthus Reborn: A Reduced Christ

A Christ Made Smaller

In every generation, there are people who claim to honor Jesus but quietly redefine Him. They speak well of His teachings, admire His compassion, and praise His example. Yet they stop short of calling Him Yehovah.

That is not new. It began in the first century with a man named Cerinthus.
He was educated, persuasive, and religious. He used the same Scriptures as the apostles but twisted their meaning. Cerinthus claimed that Yeshua was a mere man, an ordinary human who became temporarily anointed by "the Christ Spirit" at His baptism and lost it before His crucifixion.

In other words, Yeshua was not the eternal Word made flesh. He was only a moral example.

The apostle John, who personally knew Yeshua, wrote his Gospel and letters partly to expose that lie. John had encountered Cerinthus personally and rejected him outright. Early church tradition records that John once entered a public bathhouse, saw Cerinthus inside, and immediately left, saying, "Let us flee, lest the building fall, for Cerinthus, the enemy of truth, is within."[1]

John refused to share a roof with someone who denied that Yeshua was Yehovah in human form.

What Cerinthus Believed

Cerinthus grew up in Alexandria, Egypt, the same intellectual center that produced Valentinus and other Gnostic teachers. It was a city filled with philosophy, mysticism, and speculation. Blending these ideas with Scripture, Cerinthus created a system that denied the true nature of God.

He taught that:

1. The world was created not by Yehovah but by a lesser being, a demiurge, who was ignorant of the true God.
2. Yeshua was born naturally to Joseph and Mary and became righteous through His own effort.
3. "The Christ" descended on Yeshua at His baptism and empowered Him for ministry but left Him before the crucifixion.
4. Therefore, the Christ did not truly suffer or die. Only the man Yeshua did.

This separated the man from the divine, the human from the holy, and made salvation an act of human enlightenment rather than divine redemption.

Cerinthus' theology was an early attempt to make God fit human reason.

How Cerinthus Viewed Yehovah

Like Marcion, Cerinthus could not accept the God of the Hebrew Scriptures as loving and good. He viewed Yehovah as a lower, ignorant being, a craftsman who formed the physical world but had no part in the spiritual realm.

To Cerinthus, the "true" God was far above creation, detached from it, and too pure to touch matter. This was Gnostic dualism at its core, the belief that spirit is good and flesh is evil.

But this idea destroys the incarnation. If matter is evil, then the Word could not have become flesh. If Yehovah is distant, then redemption is impossible.

John opened his Gospel with a direct strike against that heresy:

"In the beginning the Word already existed. The Word was with God, and the Word was God. He existed in the beginning with God. God created everything through him, and nothing was created except through him... So the Word became human and made his home among us" (*John 1:1–3, 14, NLT*).

Every line of that passage crushes the teaching of Cerinthus.

John declared that the same God who created the world entered it. The Creator did not send someone else. He came Himself.

The Spirit of Cerinthus Today

Cerinthus may be gone, but his theology has not died. It reappears in every movement that reduces Yeshua to less than divine.

It is found in modern liberal theology that calls Jesus a moral reformer but not God. It surfaces in academic circles that praise His ethics but deny His miracles. It appears in religious groups that call Him a prophet, a teacher, or a created being but refuse to confess Him as Yehovah.

THE RISE OF MARCION AND THE FALL OF THE FAITHFUL

The apostle John wrote, "Such a person has the spirit of the Antichrist, which you heard is coming into the world and indeed is already here" (*1 John 4:3, NLT*).

He did not use that word carelessly. To John, denying Yeshua's divine identity was not a minor error. It was rebellion against truth itself.

Why the Incarnation Matters

If Yeshua was not Yehovah in the flesh, then the cross loses its power.
A mere man cannot bear the sins of the world. Only the Creator can redeem His creation.

If Yeshua was only a prophet, His blood has no eternal value. If He was only a man, His resurrection is a myth. But if He is Yehovah in the flesh, then the cross is the intersection of heaven and earth, mercy and justice, Creator and creation.

Paul wrote, "For in Christ lives all the fullness of God in a human body" (*Colossians 2:9, NLT*).

That verse alone ends the debate. The fullness of God, not a fragment or reflection, dwelled bodily in Yeshua.

A Modern Cerinthian Church

Many modern churches speak about Jesus often but rarely about His divinity. They emphasize His kindness, His teachings, His compassion, and His miracles, but they seldom proclaim that He is Yehovah, the eternal Word who created all things.

THE RISE OF MARCION AND THE FALL OF THE FAITHFUL

That silence is dangerous. It produces a powerless gospel that comforts but cannot transform.

The Church cannot settle for a smaller Jesus. A reduced Christ cannot save anyone.

Truth That Transforms

John wrote his first epistle to protect believers from Cerinthus' influence. He said, "The Son of God came to destroy the works of the devil" (*1 John 3:8, NLT*). That statement only has meaning if the Son is truly divine.

Yeshua is not a messenger of salvation. He is salvation Himself. He is not one of many paths to God. He is the only way to God because He is God.

When Philip said, "Lord, show us the Father," Yeshua replied, "Anyone who has seen me has seen the Father" (*John 14:8–9, NLT*).

That truth leaves no room for half measures.

The Faith Once Delivered

The early Church fought to preserve this confession: that Yeshua is Yehovah in the flesh. Ignatius of Antioch, a disciple of John, wrote, "There is one Physician, both fleshly and spiritual, born and unborn, God in man, true life in death, both of Mary and of God."[2]

That is the faith once delivered to the saints.

THE RISE OF MARCION AND THE FALL OF THE FAITHFUL

Every generation must defend it again. When the Church preaches a Christ who is only human, it repeats the error of Cerinthus. When it divides the divine from the human, it separates the very mystery that saves us.

True faith proclaims that Yehovah Himself took on flesh, lived among us, died for us, and rose again.

For a deeper dive into this truth, including a full study through the Gospel of Mark showing how Yeshua is revealed as Yehovah in every chapter, see my book *Mark My Words: Yeshua is Yehovah*. It explores how the earliest Gospel boldly declares the divinity of the Messiah in the simplest and clearest way possible.

Reflection Questions

1. Why is it dangerous to think of Yeshua as only a moral teacher?
2. How does denying His divinity weaken the message of the cross?
3. What passages of Scripture best show that Yeshua is Yehovah in the flesh?

Key Scriptures (NLT)

- John 1:1–14
- Colossians 2:9
- John 14:8–9
- 1 John 4:3

- 1 John 3:8

Primary Sources for Footnotes

1. Irenaeus, *Against Heresies* 3.3.4; cited by Eusebius, *Ecclesiastical History* 4.14.6.

2. Ignatius of Antioch, *Letter to the Ephesians* 7.2, in *Apostolic Fathers* (public domain).

Chapter 11 Marcion's Bible in the Modern Church

When the Church Cuts Itself in Half

If Cerinthus tried to make Yeshua smaller, Marcion tried to make the Bible smaller.
He divided it, trimmed it, and left only the parts that fit his theology.

Most Christians today would never dream of cutting books out of Scripture, but many live as if half the Bible no longer applies. They quote the New Testament with passion but avoid the Old as if it were written by a different God.

This quiet division has become so normal that few notice it anymore. Yet it is the same split Marcion made in the second century.

He believed the God of the Old Testament was cruel, and the God of the New Testament was kind.
He saw wrath and grace as opposites instead of as two sides of the same love.

That mindset never died. It simply got baptized into modern theology.

The Roots of the Divide

Marcion's influence survived long after his followers disappeared. His ideas became buried inside centuries of tradition, shaping how people read and preach the Word.

THE RISE OF MARCION AND THE FALL OF THE FAITHFUL

1. Replacement Theology carried his spirit when it taught that the Church had replaced Israel as God's chosen people. The promises of the Old Testament were "spiritualized," while the people of Israel were set aside.
   Paul directly refuted that thinking in *Romans 11:1 (NLT)*:

   "I ask, then, has God rejected his own people, the nation of Israel? Of course not! I myself am an Israelite, a descendant of Abraham and a member of the tribe of Benjamin."

2. Dispensationalism arose later as a reaction, but it too drew an invisible line between Old and New. It taught that God works with different groups in different ages and that the Law was for one age while grace is for another.
   While dispensational teachers sincerely wanted to protect grace, the framework still carried Marcion's echo, a separation between the God of Sinai and the God of Calvary.

3. Modern Grace Theology takes the same path when it treats Torah as obsolete. It claims that believers are "free from the law," yet forgets that Paul said, "We uphold the Torah" (*Romans 3:31, TLV*).

Whenever the Church treats the Hebrew Scriptures as expired, it repeats Marcion's error in a new form.

The Old Testament Problem

Many churches today preach that the Old Testament is a record of failed attempts to please God.
They speak of it as though the cross erased everything that came before.

THE RISE OF MARCION AND THE FALL OF THE FAITHFUL

But Yeshua said the exact opposite:

"Don't misunderstand why I have come. I did not come to abolish the law of Moses or the writings of the prophets. No, I came to accomplish their purpose" (*Matthew 5:17, NLT*).

He did not erase the story. He finished it.
He did not cancel the covenant. He confirmed it.

When pastors say, "We are a New Testament church," as if that means the Old no longer matters, they unknowingly echo Marcion's theology.

The truth is simple but often overlooked: the Bible Yeshua and the apostles used was what we now call the Old Testament. Every sermon they preached came from it. Every prophecy fulfilled in Yeshua came from it. Every doctrine they taught rested on it.

When Peter stood up on the day of Pentecost and preached to thousands, he did not quote Matthew, Mark, Luke, or John. None of those books had been written yet. He quoted *Joel 2* and *Psalm 16*. When Stephen gave his defense before the Sanhedrin, he told Israel's story straight from the Torah and the Prophets. When Paul reasoned with Jews and Gentiles, he did it from *Isaiah*, *Deuteronomy*, and *Psalms*.

Those were their Scriptures.
Those were their proof texts.

It would be more than twenty years after the resurrection before Paul's letters began circulating among the congregations, and decades before the Gospels were recorded. The early Church lived, taught, and proclaimed the gospel straight from what we now call the "Old Testament."

THE RISE OF MARCION AND THE FALL OF THE FAITHFUL

By the time Peter wrote his second epistle, probably between AD 64–67, many of Paul's letters were already known and recognized as inspired. Peter even called them *Scripture*:

"Our beloved brother Paul also wrote to you with the wisdom God gave him... speaking of these things in all his letters. Some of his comments are hard to understand, and those who are ignorant and unstable have twisted his letters to mean something quite different, just as they do with other parts of Scripture" (*2 Peter 3:15–16, NLT*).

That is one of the most remarkable statements in the New Testament. It shows that the apostles themselves saw Paul's writings as carrying the same divine authority as the Law and the Prophets. But it also reminds us that the foundation they stood on was still the Hebrew Scriptures.

There was no "New Testament" yet, only the living testimony of Yeshua and the written Word of Moses, David, and Isaiah.

So when Paul said in *Acts 24:14*, "I worship the God of our ancestors, and I firmly believe the Jewish law and everything written in the prophets" (*NLT*), he was describing the same Bible Yeshua used.

When you open the Old Testament, you are reading the same Scriptures that shaped the faith of the apostles. The same verses they used to prove who Messiah was still speak today.

The more you understand that, the more you realize how impossible it is to separate the New from the Old. They are not two competing revelations. They are one unfolding story of Yehovah redeeming His people through Yeshua, His Word made flesh.

THE RISE OF MARCION AND THE FALL OF THE FAITHFUL

A Divided Gospel

When we disconnect the New Testament from the Old, we lose context for everything Yeshua said and did.

We lose the meaning of the feasts, the sacrifices, the priesthood, and the covenants.
We lose the rhythm of God's redemption story.
We lose the fact that grace was present at the giving of the Torah on Mount Sinai. The people had just broken the second commandment, making a golden calf to represent Yehovah after the manner of the pagans. They should have died that day for their rebellion. Yet God, full of mercy, forgave them and renewed His covenant. That was not law without grace. That was grace giving the Law.
And eventually, we lose the gospel's foundation.

Paul warned that this would happen:

"For the time is coming when people will no longer listen to sound and wholesome teaching. They will follow their own desires and will look for teachers who will tell them whatever their itching ears want to hear" (*2 Timothy 4:3, NLT*).

Modern theology often caters to comfort. It keeps the promises but discards the commands.
 It celebrates Yeshua's love but ignores His authority.

That is Marcion's gospel in new clothes.

Paul and Tertullian's Answer

The early Church did not let Marcion's teaching go unchallenged. Tertullian wrote five volumes *Against Marcion* to prove that the

Old and New Testaments speak with one voice.
He said, "The God of the Gospel is the same as the God of the Law; both goodness and severity are found in Him."[1]

Paul made the same case in *Ephesians 2:11–22*. He showed that Jew and Gentile were not divided by two different gods or two separate covenants but united by one Savior.

"For Christ himself has brought peace to us. He united Jews and Gentiles into one people when, in his own body on the cross, he broke down the wall of hostility that separated us" (*Ephesians 2:14, NLT*).

Marcion built walls where Yeshua tore them down.

How the Modern Church Repeats Him

Many Christians read the New Testament as if God changed His mind about how He wants people to live. They say, "The law was impossible," as if that means Yehovah failed and had to try again.

But Scripture says, "The law of the Lord is perfect, reviving the soul" (*Psalm 19:7, NLT*).
What failed was not the law but our hearts.
That is why the New Covenant promise in *Jeremiah 31:33 (NLT)* says, "I will put my instructions deep within them, and I will write them on their hearts."

Even Moses told the people the same truth centuries earlier.

"This command I am giving you today is not too difficult for you to understand, and it is not beyond your reach" (*Deuteronomy 30:11, NLT*).

"No, the message is very close at hand; it is on your lips and in your heart so that you can obey it" (*Deuteronomy 30:14, NLT*).

So the Torah was never given as an impossible burden. It was a revelation of God's heart for His people. What Israel lacked was not ability but willingness.

Yet some popular grace teaching today uses *Galatians 5:4* to say the opposite.

"For if you are trying to make yourselves right with God by keeping the law, you have been cut off from Christ! You have fallen away from God's grace" (*Galatians 5:4, NLT*).

Joseph Prince teaches that "falling from grace is to go back to the Ten Commandments."[2]

Andy Stanley has said, "Peter, James, Paul elected to unhitch the Christian faith from their Jewish Scriptures, and my friends, we must as well."[3]
In another sermon, he added, "Your whole house of Old Testament cards can come tumbling down. The question is, did Jesus rise from the dead?"[4]

Even **Greg Locke** has publicly declared that "Sabbath-keeping is a demonic doctrine."[5]

Statements like these are more than rhetorical extremes. They echo the same impulse behind Marcion's teaching ... a desire to disconnect grace from the God who gave the Law.

But that is not what Paul was saying. Paul was warning Gentile believers not to rely on Torah as the basis of their justification. He was not saying Torah was bad. In fact, he said,

THE RISE OF MARCION AND THE FALL OF THE FAITHFUL

"Do we then make void the law through faith? Certainly not! On the contrary, we establish the law" (*Romans 3:31, NKJV*).

When a preacher says, "If you try to keep God's commandments you are falling from grace," that teaching slips very close to Marcion's logic. It treats the law as the enemy of grace instead of the thing grace empowers us to walk in.

It also ignores the story of Exodus. At Sinai the people made a golden calf, breaking the covenant almost the moment it was given. They should have died right then. Instead, God forgave, renewed the covenant, and kept walking with them. That is grace at the giving of the Law, not grace after the Law failed.

The covenant changed location, not content.
What was once written by the finger of God on tablets of stone is now written by His Spirit on the tablets of our hearts and minds. The same Torah - <u>the same **nomos**</u> - that once rested inside the Ark of the Covenant now rests inside His people. The difference is not the law itself but where it lives. The external became internal. The command became communion.

That is the New Covenant Jeremiah prophesied and the writer of Hebrews confirmed:

"This is the covenant that I will make with the house of Israel after those days, says the Lord: I will put My laws in their mind and write them on their hearts; and I will be their God, and they shall be My people" (*Hebrews 8:10, NKJV*).

So when modern teachers claim that obedience is bondage or that the Old Testament no longer applies, they are not preaching Paul's gospel. They are preaching a modernized version of Marcion's.

THE RISE OF MARCION AND THE FALL OF THE FAITHFUL

Restoring the Whole Bible

The only cure for a divided gospel is to return to the whole Word of God.
Both the Torah and the Testimony, the Prophets and the Apostles, speak of one Redeemer and one plan.

The Bible is not a tale of two gods or two systems. It is one story told by one Author through one Spirit.

The same God who commanded "Be holy, because I am holy" (*Leviticus 11:44, NLT*) is the same One who said, "If you love Me, obey My commandments" (*John 14:15, NLT*).

He never changed. His character did not evolve. His plan did not fail.
The same Yehovah who thundered at Sinai hung on a cross at Golgotha.

That truth restores the power of Scripture.

Why This Matters Now

A Church that ignores half its Bible cannot walk in the fullness of truth.
It becomes easy prey for confusion, false teaching, and cultural compromise.

The modern Church is drowning in Marcion's legacy. It loves grace but resents obedience. It celebrates the cross but forgets the covenant.

The only way forward is repentance.
We must stop dividing what God has united and start reading the

THE RISE OF MARCION AND THE FALL OF THE FAITHFUL

Bible as Yeshua did - as one seamless revelation of His heart, His justice, and His mercy.

Reflection Questions

1. How does modern Christianity still reflect Marcion's separation of law and grace?
2. Why is it important to read both Testaments as one story?
3. What can you do personally to reconnect your faith to the whole Word of God?

Key Scriptures

- Matthew 5:17
- Acts 24:14
- 2 Peter 3:15–16
- Romans 3:31 (NKJV)
- Ephesians 2:11–22
- Romans 11:1
- Psalm 19:7
- Jeremiah 31:33
- John 14:15
- Leviticus 11:44
- Deuteronomy 30:11–14
- Galatians 5:4
- Hebrews 8:10

Primary Sources

1. Tertullian, *Against Marcion*, Book 4, in *Ante-Nicene Fathers*, Vol. 3 (Edinburgh: T & T Clark, 1885).

2. Joseph Prince, *Destined to Reign* (Harrison House Inc., 2007), p. 128.

3. Andy Stanley, "Aftermath, Part 3: Not Difficult," North Point Community Church, May 13 2018. Transcript via Berean Research.

4. Andy Stanley quoted in Answers in Genesis.

5. Greg Locke, "Sabbath Keeping Is a Demonic Doctrine," Fulcrum7 News, Dec 14 2022.

Chapter 12 The Great Disconnect

The Way Before the Divide

Before doctrines were written on parchment and churches were built of stone, there was a movement called *The Way*.
It was not a denomination, and it had no headquarters. It was a living fellowship of Jews and Gentiles who followed Yeshua the Messiah as the promised Redeemer of Israel and the Savior of the world.

In the book of Acts, believers were not called "Christians" at first. They were called followers of *The Way*. The name came from Yeshua's own words:

"I am the way, the truth, and the life. No one can come to the Father except through Me" (*John 14:6, NLT*).

They never called themselves "Christians." That title first appears in *Acts 11:26*, when outsiders in Antioch began referring to the disciples as *Christianos,* a Greek term meaning "belonging to Christ" or "little Christ." It was not a name they chose for themselves. It was a label others gave them, sometimes in mockery. To the believers, their identity was simpler and far more ancient. They were followers of *The Way,* a path of life marked by repentance, faith, obedience, and love.

They walked in His way by obeying His commandments, loving one another, and keeping faith with the Scriptures that foretold Him. Their worship grew out of the synagogue and the Temple. Their prayers were rooted in the Psalms. Their holy days were still Yehovah's appointed times.

THE RISE OF MARCION AND THE FALL OF THE FAITHFUL

They trusted in Yeshua as their Messiah and in His sacrifice for their justification, a salvation they could never earn and received freely by faith. Yet they continued keeping Torah as their way of sanctification, living in daily obedience to God's instructions and relying on grace whenever they failed. Their faith did not make the Law void; it gave it meaning. Grace did not replace holiness; it empowered it.

When Gentiles began joining the movement, the apostles did not invent a new religion. They welcomed new believers into Israel's story. Peter called them "a chosen people, a royal priesthood, a holy nation" (*1 Peter 2:9, NLT*). Paul reminded Gentile disciples that they were once "excluded from citizenship among the people of Israel," but through Messiah they had been "brought near by the blood of Christ" (*Ephesians 2:12–13, NLT*).

This was the heart of the apostolic faith, one unified family redeemed by one covenantal Lord. The first believers never imagined a faith divorced from the Torah or detached from the promises given to Abraham, Isaac, and Jacob. They saw Yeshua not as a rejection of the Law but as its fulfillment, the living Torah written in flesh.

That was the beauty of *The Way*. It was Hebraic in rhythm, prophetic in vision, and Spirit-filled in practice. It joined heaven and earth in one message: the Kingdom of God had come near.

But within a few generations, that harmony began to fade. As the movement spread across the Gentile world, cultural distance grew between Jerusalem and the new centers of the faith. Philosophers entered the pulpits. Emperors offered protection and demanded conformity. Slowly, what began as *The Way* turned into something else, a religion defined more by creeds than by covenant, more by councils than by Scripture.

THE RISE OF MARCION AND THE FALL OF THE FAITHFUL

From The Way to the Institution

When the last of the apostles died, something precious began to fade. The firsthand witnesses of Yeshua's life, death, and resurrection were gone, and the faith they had lived and preached was now in the hands of the next generation.

At first, the pattern of *The Way* continued, worship rooted in the Hebrew Scriptures, observance of the feasts, and unity between Jewish and Gentile believers. But as the movement spread westward into Rome, Alexandria, and other Gentile cities, cultural pressure began to reshape it.

Many Gentile converts admired Yeshua but wanted little to do with the Jewish people. They carried Greek and Roman ideas of philosophy, hierarchy, and civic religion into the gatherings. Over time, those influences replaced the simple, Spirit-led structure the apostles had modeled.

Ignatius of Antioch, writing around 110 AD, began to use the word *Christianity* as a distinct term to describe the faith, contrasting it with *Judaism*. He encouraged believers to break ties with the synagogue and to look to bishops as spiritual authorities. His letters reveal both zeal for Yeshua and a growing hostility toward anything perceived as "Jewish."

Justin Martyr followed not long after. In his *Dialogue with Trypho the Jew* (around 155 AD), he argued that God's covenant with Israel had been transferred to the Church. Justin still quoted the Hebrew Scriptures, but his interpretation was allegorical, shaped more by Greek philosophy than by the literal text. In his effort to win Roman respect, he distanced the faith from its Hebrew roots, saying that Christians were the "true Israel."

THE RISE OF MARCION AND THE FALL OF THE FAITHFUL

These were the first steps away from the pattern of *The Way*. What began as fellowship became institution. What began as covenant became creed.

By the second century, the Church's leadership had adopted hierarchical systems that mirrored Roman administration. The focus shifted from walking in the Spirit to preserving authority. Bishops replaced elders. Decrees replaced discipleship.

To many believers of Jewish descent, this new direction felt foreign. Their faith had always been relational, built on obedience and love. But now, the Church was becoming political, drawing lines of power and allegiance.

The growing tension eventually erupted in open hostility. After the destruction of Jerusalem in 70 AD and the Bar Kokhba revolt in 135 AD, Rome outlawed Jewish practices, and Gentile leaders saw an opportunity to separate from anything that might draw imperial suspicion. They began to redefine the Church as a purely Gentile entity.

Instead of standing with their Jewish brothers, the Church distanced itself. It forgot that Yeshua was a Jew, that the apostles were Jews, and that the Scriptures they preached were written by Jewish hands under the Spirit of Yehovah.

The unity of *The Way* fractured into division.
The olive tree that Paul described in *Romans 11* (*one tree with both natural and grafted branches*) was being sawed in half.

This was the beginning of what history would later call *the Great Disconnect*.

THE RISE OF MARCION AND THE FALL OF THE FAITHFUL

From Persecution to Power

For nearly three centuries, followers of Yeshua lived under suspicion, persecution, and occasional waves of violent oppression. They met in homes, caves, and catacombs. They prayed in secret, clung to Scripture, and often faced death for refusing to worship the Roman gods or Caesar himself.

Then came Constantine.

In 313 AD, the Emperor issued the Edict of Milan, granting legal status to Christianity throughout the empire. Overnight, the persecuted became protected. For the first time, the Church had favor with the throne, and with that favor came influence, wealth, and compromise.

At first glance, it seemed like a miracle. Centuries of bloodshed ended. Churches were built. Bishops gained authority. The faith spread faster than ever before. But beneath the surface, something deeper was shifting.

The Church that had once refused to bow to earthly power now found itself entangled with it. Faith that had thrived under fire began to cool in comfort. The purity of *The Way* gave way to the politics of religion.

Constantine wanted a unified empire, not a divided Church. To him, theology was a matter of statecraft. Disagreements about doctrine were not spiritual concerns; they were political threats. So he convened the Council of Nicaea in 325 AD, calling bishops from across the empire to settle disputes and define orthodoxy.

That council produced the Nicene Creed, a powerful confession of Yeshua's divinity, but it also marked a turning point. The faith that

THE RISE OF MARCION AND THE FALL OF THE FAITHFUL

had once been defined by Scripture and the Spirit was now defined by imperial decree.

In the years that followed, laws were passed that made faith less Hebraic and more Roman.
Sabbath observance on the seventh day was replaced with mandatory worship on the first day.
Passover, once celebrated according to the biblical calendar, was moved to align with pagan spring festivals.
Feasts appointed by Yehovah were replaced by feast days honoring saints and martyrs.

By 364 AD, the Council of Laodicea declared,

"Christians must not Judaize by resting on the Sabbath, but must work on that day; rather, honoring the Lord's Day, they shall rest, if possible, as Christians."

That single decree turned obedience into offense. What had been holy since creation was now considered heresy.

The Church had gained the world but had begun losing its soul. What had been birthed in the power of the Spirit was being reshaped by the authority of the state.

Constantine's new religion was a blend of Scripture and empire, faith and politics, conviction and convenience. It looked Christian, but it no longer reflected *The Way*.

The Legacy of Compromise

Over time, the union of Church and State produced a version of Christianity that was easier to control but harder to recognize.

THE RISE OF MARCION AND THE FALL OF THE FAITHFUL

Bishops wore imperial robes. Altars resembled Roman temples. The Hebrew names of God were replaced with Latin titles.

The simplicity of Yeshua's command, "Follow Me," was buried under layers of ceremony and hierarchy. Instead of disciples making disciples, the Church became a system making subjects.

Many sincere believers within that system still loved Yeshua and sought truth, but the structure surrounding them made it difficult to see how far they had drifted from the faith's original foundation.

By the fifth century, the institutional Church no longer resembled *The Way* at all. It had separated from its Jewish roots, outlawed the Torah's rhythms, and persecuted the very people through whom salvation had come.

And yet, Yehovah's plan never changed.
Even in the midst of compromise, He preserved a remnant, men and women who refused to let the light of truth go out.

They are the reason we still have the Scriptures.
They are the reason truth survived the empire.

The Remnant of The Way Through the Ages

Throughout history, even as the institutional Church drifted from its Hebraic foundation, Yehovah preserved a remnant. Across centuries and continents, these men and women held fast to both the commandments of God and the testimony of Yeshua (*Revelation 12:17*). Their story forms an unbroken thread from the apostles to the reformers and into our own generation of *The Way* surviving against the odds.

1st–3rd Centuries: The Apostolic Legacy

THE RISE OF MARCION AND THE FALL OF THE FAITHFUL

The faith that began in Jerusalem spread throughout the known world. Early believers, both Jewish and Gentile, kept the commandments, honored the Sabbath, and celebrated the feasts while proclaiming Yeshua as Messiah.

Church fathers like Irenaeus and Tertullian wrote against heresies but still upheld the moral authority of Torah. Yet as Gentile influence grew, replacement theology began creeping in, separating grace from obedience.

Even so, the Spirit continued to move. The Montanist movement of the late second century produced prophecy, tongues, and spontaneous worship as believers sought holiness and purity. Though later condemned by bishops who feared enthusiasm, their passion revealed a longing for the same fire that burned in the book of Acts.

4th–6th Centuries: Faith in the Shadow of Empire

When Constantine legalized Christianity in 313 AD, the Church gained status but lost much of its substance. Imperial decrees outlawed Jewish practices and shifted worship toward Roman forms.

Yet the Spirit still stirred in hidden corners. Augustine of Hippo, though an unlikely witness, later confessed that miracles still occurred and tongues were still reported among new converts, especially during baptisms (*Retractions*, Book I).

While the official Church sought power, the remnant sought purity. The faith endured in small communities who refused to abandon the Scriptures of Israel.

7th–11th Centuries: The Hidden Keepers of the Word

THE RISE OF MARCION AND THE FALL OF THE FAITHFUL

The Celtic believers of Ireland and Scotland continued observing the seventh-day Sabbath and celebrating Passover according to the biblical calendar long after Rome demanded conformity. They combined devotion to Scripture with missionary zeal, sending monks who preached repentance and lived in simplicity.

In Eastern regions, other small groups sometimes labeled "Nazarenes" or "Ebionites" maintained a form of Torah observance, honoring Yeshua as Messiah while keeping the commandments. They were misunderstood and often persecuted, but they carried the embers of *The Way* into a dark age.

12th–14th Centuries: The Waldenses and the Prophetic Flame

In the twelfth century, the Waldenses emerged in the mountain valleys of northern Italy and southern France. They translated the Bible into common languages, rejected indulgences, and lived by the commandments of God rather than the decrees of Rome.

They were accused of "Judaizing," a term often used for Sabbath keepers and those observing biblical feasts. Their confessions reveal reverence for both Torah and the Spirit: "The Holy Spirit is given to believers for their sanctification and strength to walk according to God's commandments."

Meanwhile, within the institutional Church, Spirit-led voices continued to rise. Hildegard of Bingen (1098–1179) experienced ecstatic visions and prophetic utterances. Vincent Ferrer (1350–1419) preached repentance across Europe, and eyewitnesses claimed people of many tongues understood him simultaneously, an echo of Pentecost.

15th–17th Centuries: The Reformation Dawns

THE RISE OF MARCION AND THE FALL OF THE FAITHFUL

When corruption reached its height, Yehovah raised up reformers. Martin Luther restored the truth of salvation by faith, John Calvin revived scriptural study, and William Tyndale gave the English-speaking world the Bible. Yet even they struggled to see the Hebraic roots still beating beneath their rediscovered doctrines.

Meanwhile, Anabaptists, Sabbatarian Reformers, and Seventh Day Baptists began returning to the commandments. They sought a purer faith, grace and obedience joined once again. Their gatherings were simple, their hearts sincere, and many were filled with the Spirit as they worshiped outside the sanctioned walls of Rome and its Protestant successors alike.

18th–19th Centuries: The Fire Rekindled

The Great Awakenings swept through Europe and America, calling people back to holiness.
Among persecuted French Huguenots (Camisards), prophecy, tongues, and spiritual song returned amid suffering.
In England, John Wesley recorded encounters of believers crying out, trembling, and uttering Spirit-led prayer. Wesley's message of holiness through grace echoed the same balance taught by the apostles.

Later, Edward Irving (1792–1834) led a revival in London that saw prophecy, healing, and tongues. Though controversial, it reignited hope that the gifts of the Spirit had not ceased.

20th Century: The Spirit Poured Out Again

In 1906, the Azusa Street Revival in Los Angeles ignited global Pentecostalism under the leadership of William J. Seymour. Believers of every background spoke in tongues, prophesied, and witnessed healings as the world rediscovered the outpouring of the Holy Spirit.

THE RISE OF MARCION AND THE FALL OF THE FAITHFUL

From that fire came the Charismatic Renewal of the 1960s, which spread into Catholic, Anglican, and Protestant churches alike. Though most of these movements did not yet reconnect with Torah, they rediscovered the power of Yehovah's Spirit, the same Spirit that empowers holiness and obedience.

Late 20th–21st Centuries: The Roots Remembered

By the late twentieth century, a new awakening began to stir, one that sought to reunite Spirit and truth, grace and obedience, faith and Torah.

Early pioneers of the Hebrew Roots movement such as Dr. Roy Blizzard, Brad Scott, Monte Judah, and Eddie Chumney began teaching believers to read Scripture through the lens of its original Hebrew context. Their work built upon earlier Messianic voices like David Baron, Alfred Edersheim, and the Hebrew Christian Alliance (founded in the 1800s), who emphasized the unity of Yeshua and Torah.

This modern restoration movement does not seek to return to rabbinic legalism but to recover the apostolic pattern, Spirit-filled believers walking in covenant obedience. Many rediscovered the Sabbath, the feasts of Yehovah, and the Hebrew names of God while also flowing in prophecy, healing, and worship.

Together, they represent a new generation of *The Way,* a revival of what was never meant to die.

A Thread Unbroken

Across two thousand years, from the apostles to today, the story of *The Way* remains one of endurance and restoration.

THE RISE OF MARCION AND THE FALL OF THE FAITHFUL

The Torah was never forgotten. The Spirit was never silent. Yehovah has always had a remnant, men and women who love Him with all their heart, soul, and strength, and who walk by His Spirit in truth.

"I will put My laws in their minds, and I will write them on their hearts; and I will be their God, and they shall be My people" (*Hebrews 8:10, NKJV*).

Even when the Church was buried in ritual or empire, the heartbeat of *The Way* continued to pulse through the faithful.
That same call now echoes again, to return to the faith once delivered to the saints, the faith of Spirit and truth, grace and Torah, word and power.

THE RISE OF MARCION AND THE FALL OF THE FAITHFUL

Part 3 The Return of the Faithful

Every generation has a remnant, men and women who refuse to bow to the idols of culture, compromise, or corruption. While others drift with the tide, they anchor themselves to the Word of Yehovah. They cling to the faith of the apostles. They walk in the power of the Spirit. They love Yeshua with undivided hearts.

Part 3 equips you to join that remnant. This is the turning point of the book. After exposing the lies of the past and the errors of the present, we return to the path Scripture has marked out from the beginning. Here you will find restoration, clarity, and courage.

This section will walk you through:

- What true repentance looks like in a deceived world
- How to discern truth from counterfeits
- How to rebuild your faith on the Apostolic pattern
- How covenant, obedience, and Spirit led power work together
- How to stand as the faithful remnant in a culture of compromise

This is a call back to the ancient paths.
A call to return to the faith that once turned the world upside down.
A call to rise, endure, and follow the Shepherd who still leads His people.

Part 3 is where the remnant finds its voice again.

Chapter 13 Come Out of Her, My People

"Then I heard another voice calling from heaven,
'Come out of her, my people. Do not take part in her sins,
or you will be punished with her.'"
(*Revelation 18:4, NLT*)

There is always a time to be still, and there is a time to move. For generations, believers have built their lives within systems that look godly on the outside but carry compromise within. It has happened in every age. The faithful often find themselves surrounded by a religion that once held truth but has now blended it with convenience, culture, and comfort.

Yeshua warned this would happen. He said that in the last days, many would be deceived, that false teachers and false messiahs would rise, and that love would grow cold. Babylon (the world's system of mixture) would not just live outside the Church but creep into its walls.

That is where we find ourselves today.
A world where religion is polished, but repentance is rare.
Where grace is preached, but obedience is mocked.
Where unity is valued more than truth.

The voice from heaven still cries, "Come out of her, My people."

The Call to Separate

When Yehovah called Abraham out of Ur, He told him to leave everything familiar. He separated him from idolatry so that He could form a covenant. In every generation since, that call has sounded again. Come out. Be separate. Be holy.

The prophets repeated it to Israel when the people blended worship of Yehovah with the practices of the nations. They were warned to come out of the mixture, to stop calling holy what was common and to stop calling common what was holy.

Paul echoed the same call when he wrote,

"Come out from among them and be separate, says the Lord. Do not touch what is unclean, and I will receive you" (*2 Corinthians 6:17, NLT*).

The pattern has never changed. God's people are called out of compromise before they are called into revival.

Babylon Then and Now

In Scripture, "Babylon" represents more than a city. It is the symbol of confusion, mixture, and spiritual rebellion. In ancient Babylon, people tried to reach heaven on their own terms, building towers and idols that reflected human pride.

The same spirit of Babylon lives on in modern religion whenever we try to reshape God's Word to fit the culture, when we worship success instead of holiness, or when we trade revelation for entertainment.

Today, Babylon looks like a church that has adopted the world's methods to draw a crowd but lost the courage to preach repentance. It looks like faith that embraces the language of love while rejecting the authority of truth.

THE RISE OF MARCION AND THE FALL OF THE FAITHFUL

Revelation's warning is not just for the future ... it is for now. The call to "come out of her" is a call to leave spiritual compromise before judgment falls.

The Remnant Must Arise

Throughout history, Yehovah has always preserved a remnant. Noah stood alone in his generation. Elijah thought he was the last prophet left, yet God told him there were still seven thousand who had not bowed to Baal. During the exile, Daniel, Hananiah, Mishael, and Azariah refused to eat Babylon's food or bow to its idols.

The same kind of remnant exists today.
They are ordinary men and women who love the truth more than reputation, who would rather be faithful than fashionable.
They are leaving the noise of modern Babylon for the simplicity of devotion to Yeshua.

You can see it everywhere.
In living rooms where small groups gather to study Scripture instead of celebrity sermons.
In believers rediscovering the beauty of the Sabbath and the feasts of Yehovah.
In churches where prayer and repentance are returning to the altar.

These are not trends. They are the beginning of a return, the return of the faithful.

THE RISE OF MARCION AND THE FALL OF THE FAITHFUL

Truth Requires Separation

True repentance always involves separation. When Israel came out of Egypt, they had to leave the idols behind. When they entered covenant at Sinai, they had to choose holiness over habit. When Yeshua called His disciples, He told them to leave everything and follow Him.

The same call still stands.
You cannot cling to Babylon and walk in *The Way* at the same time.

To come out of her means to step away from anything that corrupts the truth of Scripture. It means letting go of teachings that separate grace from obedience, of churches that treat Torah as a burden instead of a gift, of systems that silence the Spirit in the name of order.

Separation does not mean isolation. We are still called to love the lost, to serve the broken, and to shine as light. But it does mean we no longer participate in what God calls unclean.

A Moment of Decision

The voice in Revelation is still speaking. It is a voice of mercy, not condemnation. God calls His people out because He is about to pour out judgment on the systems that have defiled His name.

He is calling His people to purify their worship, to rebuild their foundations, and to return to His Word.

Now is the time to decide.
Will we stay in Babylon's comfort, or will we step into the refining fire of obedience?
Will we cling to tradition, or will we walk again in *The Way*?

THE RISE OF MARCION AND THE FALL OF THE FAITHFUL

Yeshua said,

"My sheep listen to My voice; I know them, and they follow Me" (*John 10:27, NLT*).

Those who hear His voice are moving. They are leaving compromise behind. They are coming out of Babylon and back into covenant.

The Faithful Will Stand

The world will not understand this call.
Some churches will dismiss it as legalism. Others will mock it as fanaticism. But those who hear will know that it is love, more specifically ... Yehovah's love calling His children home.

The faithful remnant will rise, not by might or by power, but by His Spirit.
They will be few, but they will be pure.
They will walk in the old paths, where the good way is, and they will find rest for their souls.

"Come out of her, My people."
The voice is calling again.

This is the beginning of restoration.
The return of the faithful has begun.

Chapter 14 Testing the Doctrine

"Dear friends, do not believe everyone who claims to speak by the Spirit. You must test them to see if the Spirit they have comes from God, for there are many false prophets in the world."
(*1 John 4:1, NLT*)

The call to "come out of her" is not a call to run from every church that has flaws. It is a call to discernment, to test everything by the Word of God. Every movement, every doctrine, and every teacher must stand before Scripture.

The believers in Berea were called noble because they tested Paul's words daily against the Scriptures. That same standard still applies. In an age when feelings often replace truth, it is time to return to the discipline of testing the doctrine.

Yeshua warned that false messiahs and false prophets would arise. The apostles saw them in their own day. The early Church fought against heresies that still exist, only now they wear modern clothes. To recognize them, we have to know what they look like.

The Test of Doctrine

Below is a simple checklist of questions every believer should ask about their congregation, their teachers, and even their own beliefs. Each question connects to an ancient heresy and shows how Scripture corrects it.

THE RISE OF MARCION AND THE FALL OF THE FAITHFUL

1. Does this church reject or ignore the Tanakh?

Ancient Source: *Marcion of Sinope (2nd century)*
Patristic Refutation: *Tertullian, Against Marcion, Book 4*

Marcion rejected the entire Old Testament, claiming the God of Israel was harsh and different from the God revealed in Yeshua. He kept only a shortened version of Luke and a few edited letters of Paul that removed references to the Law and to Israel.

That same spirit lives on today when churches claim the "Old Testament" no longer applies or when pastors say that we need to unhitch from it.

Scriptural Correction:

"All Scripture is inspired by God and is useful to teach us what is true and to make us realize what is wrong in our lives." (*2 Timothy 3:16, NLT*)

Paul wrote this before the New Testament existed. To him, "All Scripture" meant the Torah, the Prophets, and the Writings. Rejecting the Tanakh is rejecting the very foundation of the faith.

---

2. Does it teach grace without obedience?

Ancient Source: *Nicolas of Antioch (1st century)*
Patristic Refutation: *Irenaeus, Against Heresies 1.26*

The Nicolaitans taught a kind of grace that excused sin. They believed believers could participate in idolatry and immorality because they were free from the Law. Revelation 2 shows that Yeshua Himself hated their deeds.

THE RISE OF MARCION AND THE FALL OF THE FAITHFUL

Today, this same deception appears in teachings that claim grace removes the need for obedience or that salvation means sin no longer matters.

Scriptural Correction:

"And we can be sure that we know him if we obey his commandments. If someone claims, 'I know God,' but doesn't obey God's commandments, that person is a liar and is not living in the truth." (*1 John 2:3–4, NLT*)

Grace is not permission to sin. It is power to overcome it.

---

3. Does it treat Yeshua as less than Yehovah?

Ancient Source: *Cerinthus (late 1st–early 2nd century)*
Patristic Refutation: *Irenaeus, Against Heresies 1.26; Eusebius, Church History 3.28*

Cerinthus taught that Yeshua was only a man who temporarily received the "Christ Spirit." He denied that Yeshua was divine and that the Word had become flesh.

Modern versions of this error appear whenever Yeshua is reduced to a moral teacher, a prophet, or a created being instead of being recognized as Yehovah in the flesh.

Scriptural Correction:

"In the beginning the Word already existed. The Word was with God, and the Word was God." (*John 1:1, NLT*)
"For in Christ lives all the fullness of God in a human body." (*Colossians 2:9, NLT*)

To deny Yeshua's full divinity is to deny the core of salvation itself.

THE RISE OF MARCION AND THE FALL OF THE FAITHFUL

4. Does it elevate secret knowledge or the leader's revelations?

Ancient Source: *Valentinus (2nd century)*
Patristic Refutation: *Irenaeus, Against Heresies, Book 1*

Valentinus built a movement around secret revelation. He taught that only those with "gnosis," or special knowledge, could understand the deep truths of God. This created a class of spiritual elites and produced pride instead of humility.

The same error appears today when leaders claim only their group has "the real revelation" or when a pastor's visions carry the same weight as Scripture.

Scriptural Correction:

"Don't let anyone condemn you by insisting on pious self-denial or the worship of angels, saying they have had visions about these things. Their sinful minds have made them proud." (*Colossians 2:18, NLT*)

True revelation never contradicts Scripture. The Holy Spirit confirms truth. He does not replace it.

5. Does it disconnect the Church from Israel?

Ancient Source: *Justin Martyr (2nd century)* and later teachers of Replacement Theology
Patristic Refutation: *Tertullian, Against Marcion 5; Romans 11*

Justin Martyr claimed that God had transferred His covenant from Israel to the Church. This became the root of replacement theology,

THE RISE OF MARCION AND THE FALL OF THE FAITHFUL

which taught that Israel was forsaken and that the Church was now the "true Israel."

This false idea still shapes much of modern theology. It denies the eternal covenant and blinds believers to Israel's ongoing role in Yehovah's redemptive plan.

Scriptural Correction:

"Did God's people stumble and fall beyond recovery? Of course not! Some of the branches from Abraham's tree have been broken off, and you Gentiles, who were branches from a wild olive tree, have been grafted in." (*Romans 11:11–17, NLT*)

We were grafted in, not grafted over. The root is still Israel.

---

6. Does it change or cut Scripture?

Ancient Source: *Marcion and his followers*
Patristic Refutation: *Tertullian, Against Marcion, Book 4*

Marcion edited Scripture to remove anything that disagreed with his ideas. He literally cut out verses from Luke and Paul's letters. Today, this happens when people ignore passages that challenge their beliefs or twist Scripture to fit cultural trends.

Scriptural Correction:

"Every word of God proves true. He is a shield to all who come to him for protection. Do not add to his words, or he may rebuke you and expose you as a liar." (*Proverbs 30:5–6, NLT*)

Truth does not need editing. If our beliefs require cutting or changing Scripture, then our beliefs are wrong, not the Word.

THE RISE OF MARCION AND THE FALL OF THE FAITHFUL

Testing the Fruit

Right doctrine always produces right living. Yeshua said we would know false teachers by their fruit. If a teaching produces pride, confusion, or lawlessness, it is not from Him. If it produces humility, obedience, and love, it carries His Spirit.

Testing doctrine is not an act of suspicion. It is an act of devotion. It shows that we value truth enough to guard it.

"Examine yourselves to see if your faith is genuine. Test yourselves." (*2 Corinthians 13:5, NLT*)

The early Church faced all these heresies, and the faithful remnant stood firm by clinging to the Word. We are called to do the same.

When you test doctrine, you are not dividing the body. You are protecting it.

THE RISE OF MARCION AND THE FALL OF THE FAITHFUL

Chapter 15 Returning to the Ancient Path

"Don't misunderstand why I have come. I did not come to abolish the law of Moses or the writings of the prophets. No, I came to accomplish their purpose."
(Matthew 5:17, NLT)

Every generation of believers eventually faces the same crossroads. We either keep walking in the path God laid before us, or we drift into newer ideas that promise freedom but lead us into confusion. When the foundation beneath our feet begins to crack, when our faith starts to lean, and when modern theology pulls us in different directions, we have to stop and return to the ancient path.

Not nostalgia. Not tradition.
The path laid by God Himself.
The path walked by Abraham, Moses, David, the prophets, the apostles, and by Yeshua our Messiah.

The Church cannot stand strong on a foundation of half-truths or borrowed philosophies. We have to return to what the apostles taught and how they lived. They did not see the Torah as bondage or the Spirit as a substitute for obedience. They saw both as essential to the life of every believer.

The Word and the Spirit Together

From the beginning, God's plan was for His Word and His Spirit to work together. In creation, the Spirit of God hovered over the waters while His Word brought order and life. At Mount Sinai, the

THE RISE OF MARCION AND THE FALL OF THE FAITHFUL

Torah was spoken by the voice of God, and at Pentecost, the Spirit was poured out to write that same law on human hearts.

Paul explained this balance clearly.

Romans 3:31 (NKJV):
"Do we then make void the law through faith? Certainly not. On the contrary, we establish the law."

Faith does not replace obedience.
Faith empowers obedience.
Faith gives it meaning and strength.

The covenant changed location, not content. What was written on stone is now written on the heart by the Holy Spirit. The same instructions that defined holiness then still reveal holiness now.

The Early Believers Understood This

The early believers never saw a conflict between grace and obedience. They understood that salvation is a gift through faith, but that true faith produces obedience. The apostles did not divide the Scriptures into old and new. They preached one continuous revelation of God's plan.

When the apostles preached, their Bible was the Tanakh. Every sermon, prophecy, and moral instruction they gave came from what we now call the Old Testament.

Yeshua Himself quoted Deuteronomy, Psalms, and Isaiah more than any other books. When He faced temptation in the wilderness, He did not rely on emotion or opinion. He answered Satan with the written Word, saying, "It is written."

THE RISE OF MARCION AND THE FALL OF THE FAITHFUL

The same Spirit who inspired the prophets inspired the apostles. There was never a contradiction between the two.

The Witness of the Early Fathers

Even after the apostles, the early Church fathers still recognized the unity of Scripture.

Tertullian wrote in *Against Marcion* that "The law and the gospel are not contrary, but harmonious, since both come from one and the same God." He argued that Yeshua fulfilled the Torah's promises, not abolished them.

Irenaeus declared in *Against Heresies* that "Christ did not do away with the natural precepts of the law, but extended and fulfilled them." He understood that the moral foundation of Torah is eternal because it reflects God's unchanging nature.

These men, living only a generation or two after the apostles, knew the Word and Spirit could not be separated. They warned that the heresies of their day came from people who rejected the Torah and replaced it with philosophy or human tradition.

Restoring the Balance

Modern Christianity often swings between two extremes. Some cling to the Word but deny the Spirit, producing religion without power. Others pursue the Spirit but ignore the Word, producing emotion without truth.

The apostles did neither.
They lived by both.

THE RISE OF MARCION AND THE FALL OF THE FAITHFUL

The Torah reveals God's character.
The Spirit empowers us to walk it out.

Without the Torah, we have no definition of righteousness.
Without the Spirit, we lack the strength to live it.

Hebrews 8:10 (NLT):
"This is the covenant that I will make with the house of Israel after those days, says the Lord. I will put My laws in their minds and write them on their hearts."

This is what restoration looks like. Not a return to the letter that kills, but to the Spirit who gives life through obedience from the heart.

The Foundation of the Apostles

Acts describes the early community of believers as:

Acts 2:42 (NLT):
"They devoted themselves to the apostles' teaching and to fellowship and to sharing in meals and to prayer."

Their foundation was solid.
They had doctrine rooted in Scripture.
They had community filled with love.
They had power supplied by the Holy Spirit.

That is the foundation we are called to restore.
A faith built on the Word.
A life led by the Spirit.
A people walking in holiness and love.

THE RISE OF MARCION AND THE FALL OF THE FAITHFUL

When we return to the ancient path, the same power that turned the world upside down in the first century will transform our generation again.

THE RISE OF MARCION AND THE FALL OF THE FAITHFUL

Chapter 16 Walking in the Way

"All the believers devoted themselves to the apostles' teaching, and to fellowship, and to sharing in meals, including the Lord's Supper, and to prayer."
(*Acts 2:42, NLT*)

When the Holy Spirit was poured out at Pentecost, it did not create a new religion. It gave new life to the faith that had always been there. The same God who spoke at Sinai now wrote His law on human hearts. The people of *The Way* were not inventing a different path; they were finally walking in the one God had always intended.

Walking in *The Way* means more than believing the right things. It means living the right way. The first believers showed us how. Their lives were simple, powerful, and full of love for both God and each other.

They Devoted Themselves to the Word

The first believers were devoted to the apostles' teaching. Those teachings were not new doctrines but explanations of the Torah and Prophets that revealed Yeshua as the promised Messiah.

They studied together daily. They read Scripture aloud. They memorized it, prayed it, and applied it. The Word was their foundation.

THE RISE OF MARCION AND THE FALL OF THE FAITHFUL

In every generation, revival begins the same way. When God's people return to the Word with open hearts, the Spirit breathes life into the pages. Understanding becomes transformation.

They Lived in Fellowship

The community of *The Way* was built on relationship, not ritual. They shared meals, cared for one another, and met needs within the family of faith. No one claimed that what they owned was theirs alone.

Fellowship was more than social connection. It was covenant loyalty. When one believer suffered, others came alongside. When one rejoiced, all rejoiced.

Yeshua said, "Your love for one another will prove to the world that you are my disciples." (*John 13:35, NLT*) That love was visible. It was generous. It was holy.

They Practiced Holiness

To walk in *The Way* meant to walk in obedience. The early believers understood that grace did not free them from the commandments but empowered them to live them out.

They honored the Sabbath as a day of rest and worship. They observed the feasts of Yehovah as reminders of His redemption plan. They avoided idolatry and immorality, not because of rules, but because they loved the One who had redeemed them.

The Spirit was their helper. When they stumbled, grace lifted them. When they obeyed, the Spirit filled them with joy.

THE RISE OF MARCION AND THE FALL OF THE FAITHFUL

Holiness was not a burden. It was freedom from sin's control.

They Prayed with Power

Prayer was the heartbeat of the early Church. They prayed in homes, in the Temple courts, and on the streets. They prayed in faith, believing that God still heals, delivers, and saves.

The same Spirit that spoke through the prophets now spoke through them. Prophecy, tongues, and miracles were not special privileges for the apostles; they were evidence that the same God who parted the sea was still at work among His people.

When they prayed, the earth shook. Chains broke. Hearts turned. The Spirit moved because the people were willing.

They Shared What They Had

Generosity was another mark of *The Way*. Those who had resources gave freely to those in need. The community did not rely on coercion or guilt; they gave because love compelled them.

In doing so, they fulfilled the Torah's command to care for the poor and the stranger. Obedience and compassion worked together.

They Walked in Joy

The book of Acts says that they ate their meals with gladness and simplicity of heart, praising God and enjoying the goodwill of all the people. Joy was not dependent on circumstances. It came from knowing they were walking in truth.

THE RISE OF MARCION AND THE FALL OF THE FAITHFUL

That same joy is available today. When believers live by both Word and Spirit, they find peace that the world cannot take away.

Returning to The Way

The call to return to *The Way* is not a call to nostalgia. It is a call to renewal. It is not about going backward but about recovering what was lost.

When we walk as the first believers did, our faith becomes alive again.
We begin to see miracles in everyday life.
We begin to love one another deeply.
We begin to live in holiness without pride and in grace without compromise.

This is what Yeshua meant when He said, "Follow Me."

To walk in *The Way* is to walk as He walked, filled with the Spirit, guided by the Word, and clothed in humility.

It is a life that looks different from the world because it belongs to another Kingdom.

"This is what the Lord says: 'Stand at the crossroads and look. Ask for the old, godly way, and walk in it. Travel its path, and you will find rest for your souls.'"
(*Jeremiah 6:16, NLT*)

Chapter 17 Renouncing the Lies

"You will know the truth, and the truth will set you free."
(John 8:32, NLT)

Truth brings freedom. Lies bring bondage.
From the beginning, the enemy's strategy has always been deception. His goal is not only to tempt but to distort truth just enough to make it look holy while leading us away from obedience.

Renouncing lies is not about arguing theology. It is about repentance. It is a choice to remove anything that stands between us and Yehovah. It is a spiritual cleansing that allows truth to take its rightful place again.

When Israel left Egypt, they not only walked out of slavery, they left behind its gods, its customs, and its false worship. In the same way, those returning to *The Way* must leave behind the doctrines that enslaved them to compromise and confusion.

This chapter is a time to do that, to speak truth aloud, to reject error, and to realign the heart with the Word of God.

Why Renouncing Matters

Words have power. Proverbs 18:21 says, "The tongue can bring death or life."
When we repeat a lie long enough, it begins to shape what we believe. When we declare truth, it reshapes our heart and renews our mind.

THE RISE OF MARCION AND THE FALL OF THE FAITHFUL

Renouncing lies breaks agreement with false teaching. It exposes what the enemy used to keep us in spiritual darkness. Speaking God's Word over those areas invites the light of His Spirit to restore what was lost.

In Scripture, confession always brings cleansing. First John 1:9 says, "If we confess our sins to him, he is faithful and just to forgive us our sins and to cleanse us from all wickedness."

This is not a ritual. It is a moment of surrender.

How to Renounce

Find a quiet place. Ask the Holy Spirit to bring to mind any teaching, habit, or belief that is not rooted in truth. Then read each declaration below slowly and prayerfully. Speak it aloud. Do not rush.

Each statement includes a lie to reject and a truth to affirm. Let the Word of God be your authority.

Declarations of Truth

1. Concerning the Nature of God
Lie: I can follow Yeshua without fully honoring Yehovah, the God of Israel.
Truth: I serve one God, Yehovah, who revealed Himself through Yeshua the Messiah.

"Hear, O Israel: Yehovah our God, Yehovah is one." (*Deuteronomy 6:4*)
"The Father and I are one." (*John 10:30, NLT*)

THE RISE OF MARCION AND THE FALL OF THE FAITHFUL

Declaration: I reject the teaching that the God of Israel is not my God. I confess that Yeshua is Yehovah made flesh and worthy of my worship.

---

2. Concerning Grace and Obedience
Lie: Grace means I no longer need to obey God's commandments.
Truth: Grace empowers me to live in holiness and obedience to God's Word.

"Well then, should we keep on sinning so that God can show us more and more of his wonderful grace? Of course not!" (*Romans 6:1–2, NLT*)

"And we can be sure that we know him if we obey his commandments." (*1 John 2:3, NLT*)

Declaration: I reject the lie that grace replaces obedience. I believe that my justification comes only through faith in the sacrifice of Yeshua, which I could never earn. I believe that sanctification comes as I walk in His commandments through the power of the Holy Spirit.

My walk in obedience shows that my faith is a good tree and is producing good fruit. I will live in holiness through His grace and reflect His righteousness within me.

---

3. Concerning the Scriptures
Lie: The Old Testament is no longer relevant for believers today.
Truth: All Scripture is God-breathed and profitable for teaching, correction, and instruction in righteousness.

"All Scripture is inspired by God and is useful to teach us what is true." (*2 Timothy 3:16, NLT*)

Declaration: I reject the lie that the Torah has been abolished. I receive the Word of God as one continuous revelation that reveals Yeshua from beginning to end.

---

4. *Concerning Yeshua's Identity*
Lie: Yeshua was a created being or only a prophet.
Truth: Yeshua is the Word made flesh, the visible image of the invisible God.

"In the beginning the Word already existed. The Word was with God, and the Word was God." (*John 1:1, NLT*)
"For in Christ lives all the fullness of God in a human body." (*Colossians 2:9, NLT*)

Declaration: I reject any teaching that denies Yeshua's divinity. I confess that Yeshua is Yehovah in human form, my Savior and my King.

---

5. *Concerning Israel and the Church*
Lie: God has rejected Israel and replaced her with the Church.
Truth: Believers in Messiah are grafted into Israel's covenant, not separated from it.

"You Gentiles, who were branches from a wild olive tree, have been grafted in." (*Romans 11:17, NLT*)

Declaration:
I reject replacement theology and affirm that God's covenant with Israel is everlasting.
I am part of that covenant through Yeshua the Messiah.

THE RISE OF MARCION AND THE FALL OF THE FAITHFUL

I am in agreement with Paul and declare that I am now a citizen in the commonwealth of Israel.

6. *Concerning Knowledge and Revelation*
Lie: Only special teachers or movements have the real truth.
Truth: The Holy Spirit leads every believer into truth through the Word.

"When the Spirit of truth comes, he will guide you into all truth." (*John 16:13, NLT*)

Declaration: I reject pride and spiritual elitism. I will submit to the guidance of the Holy Spirit and test every revelation by Scripture.

7. *Concerning the Word of God*
Lie: Scripture can be edited, adjusted, or reinterpreted to fit modern views.
Truth: Every word of God is true, eternal, and unchanging.

"Every word of God proves true. Do not add to his words." (*Proverbs 30:5–6, NLT*)

Declaration: I reject every false teaching that alters or removes the Word of God. I will build my life upon Scripture as my only standard for truth.

A Prayer of Renewal

Father, I come before You in the name of Yeshua.
I renounce every lie that I have believed about You or Your Word.
I break agreement with false teaching and confusion.

THE RISE OF MARCION AND THE FALL OF THE FAITHFUL

I receive Your truth, written in Scripture and confirmed by Your Spirit.

Write Your Torah on my heart.
Fill me again with Your Spirit of truth.
Teach me to walk in humility, obedience, and love.
Let my life reflect the purity of *The Way* that Yeshua taught and lived.

I confess with my mouth that Yeshua is Yehovah, the Lord of all.
I belong to You, and I will walk in Your truth all my days.
Amen.

> THE RISE OF MARCION AND THE FALL OF THE FAITHFUL

Chapter 18 The Faithful Remnant

"And now to Him who is able to keep you from falling and to present you without fault before His glorious presence with great joy. All glory to Him who alone is God, our Savior through Yeshua the Messiah, our Lord. All glory, majesty, power, and authority are His before all time, and in the present, and beyond all time. Amen." (Jude 24–25, NLT)

Every generation faces the choice between compromise and faithfulness. In the days of Noah, only one family stood apart from the corruption of the world. In the time of Elijah, only seven thousand refused to bow to Baal. In Babylon, Daniel and his friends refused the king's food and worshiped only Yehovah.

In our generation, the same call echoes again.

The faithful remnant is not large or powerful in the world's eyes. They are often unseen and uncelebrated, but Heaven knows their names. They refuse to trade truth for popularity or holiness for comfort. They love Yehovah more than the praise of men.

What Defines the Remnant

The remnant are those who hear Yehovah's voice even when the world grows loud. They love His Word more than their own opinions. They live by both Spirit and truth. They honor Yeshua as Yehovah in the flesh and stand firm on His commandments with joy.

THE RISE OF MARCION AND THE FALL OF THE FAITHFUL

They do not measure success by numbers or applause but by faithfulness. Their goal is not to win arguments but to please the One who called them. They may look small, but they carry the authority of Heaven because they walk in covenant with the Living God.

Zephaniah described them this way:

"The remnant of Israel will do no wrong; they will never tell lies or deceive one another. They will eat and sleep in safety, and no one will make them afraid."
 (Zephaniah 3:13, NLT)

They are marked by purity, humility, and courage.

The Days of Refining

Yehovah always refines His people through testing. The remnant is not born through comfort but through fire. When falsehood rises and truth is despised, those who remain loyal to the Word shine like light in the darkness.

Malachi saw this clearly:

"He will sit like a refiner of silver, burning away the dross. He will purify the Levites, refining them like gold and silver, so they may once again offer acceptable sacrifices to the Lord."
(Malachi 3:3, NLT)

The refining is not punishment. It is preparation.
Yehovah is raising up a people who love Him with undivided hearts, who serve Him in spirit and in truth, and who do not bend when the winds of culture blow.

THE RISE OF MARCION AND THE FALL OF THE FAITHFUL

If you have endured the testing, you are not forgotten. You are being purified for purpose.

The Remnant's Mission

The faithful remnant is not called to hide. They are called to stand. Their mission is to guard the truth, live in love, and call others back to the ancient paths.

Jeremiah declared:

"This is what Yehovah says: Stand at the crossroads and look. Ask for the old, godly way, and walk in it. Travel its path, and you will find rest for your souls."
(Jeremiah 6:16, NLT)

This is the calling of the remnant today! To rebuild what was broken, repair the breach, and restore the foundations of faith the apostles laid.

They teach grace and obedience side by side.
They love Israel and honor her covenant.
They walk in the gifts of the Spirit while holding fast to the truth of the Word.
They live for the glory of Yehovah and the coming Kingdom of Yeshua.

A Call to Endurance

The days ahead will test faith in ways the modern Church is not prepared for. The spirit of Marcion, the pride of Gnosticism, and the compromise of the Nicolaitans have not vanished. They have only changed form. But the same God who preserved His remnant before will preserve His people again.

Yeshua warned us:

"The one who endures to the end will be saved."
(Matthew 24:13, NLT)

Endurance is not about strength. It is about faithfulness.
It is trusting Yehovah when everything around you demands surrender.
It is standing firm in truth when others fall away.

When the world mocks, endure.
When religion compromises, endure.
When the path feels narrow and lonely, endure.

You are not alone.

The Joy of the Remnant

The remnant walks in joy, not despair. They know Yeshua is coming again to establish His Kingdom and that their labor is not in vain.

Paul encouraged us:

"Dear brothers and sisters, be strong and immovable. Always work enthusiastically for the Lord, for you know that nothing you do for the Lord is ever useless."
(1 Corinthians 15:58, NLT)

The world may not understand the joy of those who walk in obedience, but Heaven celebrates it. The faithful remnant rejoices because they have found rest in the truth. Their reward is not comfort in this life but glory in the next.

A Final Prayer

Father, thank You for keeping a remnant in every generation.
Thank You for calling me out of compromise and into covenant.
Make me faithful in word, pure in heart, and steadfast in truth.
Let me walk in humility and courage until the day Yeshua returns.
Keep me from falling.
Present me before Your glorious presence with joy.
Let my life bring honor to the name of Yehovah.
To You belong all glory, majesty, power, and authority, now and forever.
Amen.

What's next???

As the world shifts and the Church drifts, the remnant must understand *why* these battles keep returning. The lies confronting believers today are not new. They were planted long ago by men who twisted Scripture, divided God's people, and attempted to rewrite the identity of Yeshua Himself.

These ancient errors have returned under new names.
They have shaped seminaries, sermons, and systems of thought.
They have produced confusion about grace, obedience, Torah, Israel, and the Gospel itself.

If we want to stand firm, we must expose these lies.
If we want to endure, we must know where they came from.
If we want to remain faithful, we must rebuild on truth.

THE RISE OF MARCION AND THE FALL OF THE FAITHFUL

That is why the next part of this book exists.

Part 4 uncovers the errors that took root in the early centuries, traces how they resurfaced in modern theology, and equips you to recognize, refute, and reject them. This is not academic. It is survival. It is discipleship. It is returning to the way Yeshua lived and the truth the apostles preached.

The remnant is rising.
Now we restore the foundations.

THE RISE OF MARCION AND THE FALL OF THE FAITHFUL

Part 4 Restoring the Foundations

There comes a moment when every believer must decide what their faith stands upon.
Tradition or truth.
Comfort or covenant.
Man-made systems or the Word of Yehovah.

Part 4 exists to rebuild what has been lost.

Here we expose the teachings that fractured the Church, divided the Scriptures, and weakened the Gospel. We will confront the ancient heresies that never died, the modern doctrines that echo them, and the lies that continue to shape much of Christianity today.

This section will walk you through:

- The heresies the apostles confronted
- The distortions Marcion introduced
- The errors that crept into the early Church
- The misused Scriptures still quoted today
- The modern system of Dispensationalism that revives Marcion's ideas

And most importantly:

We will return to the simple, unbroken truth the apostles lived and taught.

This is restoration.
This is equipping.

THE RISE OF MARCION AND THE FALL OF THE FAITHFUL

This is the foundation the remnant must stand on in the days ahead.

> THE RISE OF MARCION AND THE FALL OF THE FAITHFUL

Chapter 19 Yehovah's Compassion in the Hebrew Scriptures

Some claim Yeshua introduced compassion that did not exist in the Old Testament. The Scriptures themselves prove this false. You see Yehovah's love, patience, and tenderness woven through every part of the Hebrew Bible. Yeshua did not bring a new kind of mercy. He revealed the mercy that was already there.

This becomes clear when you look at two things:

1. **How Yehovah treats the nations**, even when they are violent.

2. **How Yehovah treats Israel**, even when they rebel.

Both expose the myth of a harsh Old Testament God.

Mercy Toward Nineveh: Compassion for the Worst of Nations

Nineveh was not a minor pagan city. It was the capital of the Assyrian Empire, one of the most violent and oppressive societies in the ancient world. Their own kings carved their brutality into stone. These were not rumors or accusations. They were royal boasts.

Historical Records of Nineveh's Cruelty

Ashurnasirpal II (883–859 BC)
"I built a pillar over against his city gate and I flayed all the chief men who had revolted, and I covered the pillar with their skins."
(Source: Pritchard, *Ancient Near Eastern Texts*, p. 276)

"I cut off the limbs of the officers who had rebelled... I burned many captives... I cut off the heads of many and formed them into a pillar."
(Source: *ANET*, p. 277)

Ashurbanipal (669–627 BC)
"I tore out the tongues of those whose slanderous mouths had uttered blasphemies. The others I smashed with stones."
(Source: *ANET*, p. 288)

"I cut off their heads and carried them to Nineveh for the entertainment of the people."
(Source: *ANET*, p. 289)

Tiglath-Pileser I (1114–1076 BC)
"I cut off the arms and hands of my enemies and displayed them."
(Source: *ANET*, p. 282)

Archaeological Reliefs From Nineveh

The palace reliefs of Sennacherib and Ashurbanipal (British Museum collections) show:

- Prisoners impaled on stakes
- Eyes being gouged out
- Hooks through lips and noses
- Piles of severed heads

THE RISE OF MARCION AND THE FALL OF THE FAITHFUL

- Families led away in chains

This was the moral climate of Nineveh when Jonah preached there.

Yet Yehovah Forgave Them

Jonah hated the idea of God forgiving these people. He said so openly:

Jonah 4:2 (NLT):
"I knew that you are a merciful and compassionate God, slow to get angry and filled with unfailing love. You are eager to turn back from destroying people."

And when Nineveh repented, God did exactly that.

Jonah 3:10 (NLT):
"When God saw what they had done and how they had put a stop to their evil ways, he changed his mind and did not carry out the destruction he had threatened."

This is the same compassion Yeshua displays in the Gospels. The idea that compassion begins in the New Testament collapses under the weight of Scripture and history.

Mercy Toward Israel: Compassion After Repeated Rebellion

Israel's history is a cycle of rebellion met with astonishing mercy. Over and over, they sin. Over and over, Yehovah forgives, restores, and redeems.

Here is a clear list of examples that reveal His patience:

THE RISE OF MARCION AND THE FALL OF THE FAITHFUL

- **The Golden Calf**
  Exodus 32:1–14; 34:6–10

- **Complaining at the Red Sea**
  Exodus 14:10–22

- **Grumbling at Marah**
  Exodus 15:22–25

- **Complaining About Food**
  Exodus 16:2–15

- **Complaining About Water at Rephidim**
  Exodus 17:1–7

- **Refusing to Enter the Promised Land**
  Numbers 14:1–20

- **Rebellion of Korah**
  Numbers 16:1–50

- **Complaining After Korah's Judgment**
  Numbers 16:41–50

- **Grumbling and the Bronze Serpent**
  Numbers 21:4–9

- **Idolatry at Baal Peor**
  Numbers 25:1–9

- **Repeated Idolatry in Judges**
  Judges 2:11–19

- **Syncretism in Samuel's Day**
  1 Samuel 7:3–12

THE RISE OF MARCION AND THE FALL OF THE FAITHFUL

- **Demanding a King Like the Nations**
  1 Samuel 8:4–22

- **Ahab's Apostasy**
  1 Kings 18; 2 Kings 2–13

- **Hezekiah's Pride and Restoration**
  2 Chronicles 32:24–26

- **Manasseh's Wickedness and Repentance**
  2 Chronicles 33:10–13

- **Post-Exilic Restoration**
  Nehemiah 9:16–31

Each of these moments shows Yehovah's compassion in action. He disciplines, but He restores. He judges, but He relents. He calls Israel back again and again because His heart is full of mercy.

He Reveals His Own Character

When Moses asks to see His glory, Yehovah reveals His very nature:

Exodus 34:6–7 (NLT):
"Yehovah! The God of compassion and mercy! I am slow to anger and filled with unfailing love and faithfulness... I forgive iniquity, rebellion, and sin."

This is the same God revealed in Yeshua. Compassion did not begin in the New Testament. It is the eternal character of Yehovah.

THE RISE OF MARCION AND THE FALL OF THE FAITHFUL

Conclusion: The Testimony Is Unavoidable

The Hebrew Scriptures show Yehovah forgiving:

- Violent nations
- Idolatrous nations
- Rebellious prophets
- Stubborn kings
- Entire generations of His people

Yeshua's compassion matches the Old Testament perfectly because He is revealing the same God Moses met on Sinai and the same God Jonah fled from.

This destroys the myth of a harsh Old Testament God. The compassion seen in Yeshua is ancient, foundational, and eternal.

THE RISE OF MARCION AND THE FALL OF THE FAITHFUL

Chapter 20 The Rejection of the Written Torah

One of the oldest and most destructive errors in Church history is the belief that the written Torah no longer matters for the people of God. Marcion turned this idea into a complete doctrine. He claimed the Hebrew Scriptures were inferior, temporary, and incompatible with the Gospel. Later movements repeated the same arguments, sometimes knowingly and sometimes not. The result has been confusion, division, and a Gospel cut loose from its foundation.

Scripture presents the opposite. Yeshua, the apostles, and the early believers viewed the written Torah as holy, good, enduring, and essential for understanding the character of Yehovah. Torah was never a ladder to climb for salvation. It was the revealed wisdom that guides the redeemed.

The problem is not Torah. The problem is how people misunderstand it.

Yeshua Affirms the Written Torah, Not Replaces It

Yeshua did not come to abolish the Torah. He said so with absolute clarity.

Matthew 5:17 to 19 (NLT):
"Don't misunderstand why I have come. I did not come to abolish the law of Moses or the writings of the prophets. No, I came to accomplish their purpose.
I tell you the truth, until heaven and earth disappear, not even the smallest detail of God's law will disappear until its purpose is

achieved.
So if you ignore the least commandment and teach others to do the same, you will be called the least in the Kingdom of Heaven."

Rejecting Torah is not spiritual progress. It is spiritual decline.

When Yeshua summed up discipleship, He quoted the Torah itself.

Matthew 22:37 to 40 (NLT):
"'You must love the Lord your God with all your heart...' This is the first and greatest commandment.
A second is equally important. 'Love your neighbor as yourself.'
The entire law and all the demands of the prophets are based on these two commandments."

He does not discard. He fulfills. He does not oppose. He clarifies.

Paul Defended the Torah Against Misuse, Not Against Itself

Marcion misread Paul, and many have repeated the same mistake. Paul never attacked Torah. He attacked the idea that Torah could save. That was never its purpose.

Romans 3:31 (NKJV):
"Do we then make void the law through faith? Certainly not. On the contrary, we establish the law."

Romans 7:12 (NLT):
"But still, the law itself is holy, and its commands are holy and right and good."

Romans 7:22 (NLT):
"I love God's law with all my heart."

THE RISE OF MARCION AND THE FALL OF THE FAITHFUL

Paul rejects misuse while affirming obedience. Salvation is by grace. The life of the redeemed is shaped by God's commands.

The Early Believers Continued to Live Torah Faithfully

The early Jewish believers did not abandon Torah. They walked in it with joy. And the Gentile believers who joined them were taught to honor it.

James and the Jerusalem Community

James describes Torah as the law of freedom.

James 1:25 (NLT):
"But if you look carefully into the perfect law that sets you free and do what it says, God will bless you for doing it."

Paul's Own Life

Paul lived Torah faithfully long after encountering Yeshua.

Acts 21:20 to 24 (NLT):
"You see, brother, how many thousands of Jews have also believed, and they all follow the law of Moses very seriously...
Then everyone will know that the rumors are all false and that you yourself observe the Jewish laws."

Paul confirms this again:

Acts 24:14 (NLT):
"I worship the God of our ancestors, and I firmly believe the Jewish law and everything written in the prophets."

Gentiles Were Expected to Learn Torah

THE RISE OF MARCION AND THE FALL OF THE FAITHFUL

The Jerusalem council did not free Gentiles from Torah. It freed them from circumcision as a requirement for salvation. The apostles connected Gentiles to synagogue teaching.

Acts 15:21 (NLT):
"For these laws of Moses have been preached in Jewish synagogues in every city on every Sabbath for many generations."

The expectation was simple. Gentiles would learn Moses every Sabbath.

The Torah Reveals the Way, the Truth, and the Life

The Scriptures describe Torah with the very titles Yeshua later applies to Himself. Torah shows the path. Torah reveals truth. Torah guards life.

The Way

Psalm 119:30 (NLT):
"I have chosen to be faithful. I have determined to live by your regulations."

The Truth

Psalm 86:11 (NLT):
"Teach me your ways, O Lord, that I may live according to your truth."

The Life

Proverbs 6:23 (NLT):
"For this command is a lamp and this teaching is a light, and correction and discipline are the way to life."

THE RISE OF MARCION AND THE FALL OF THE FAITHFUL

Yeshua's Claim

John 14:6 (NLT):
"Jesus told him, I am **the way**, **the truth**, and **the life**. No one can come to the Father except through me."

Yeshua takes the titles already spoken of Torah and applies them to Himself. He is not canceling the Torah. He is revealing the One who gave it. He is the living expression of the faithful path. He is the truth the Scriptures proclaim. He is the life the commandments protect.

Yeshua and Torah do not stand apart. They stand together. The Way found in Scripture leads to the Messiah. The Truth revealed in Torah points to Him. The Life guarded by God's commands is the life Yeshua offers. Rejecting the written Torah is rejecting the revelation Yeshua said He fulfilled.

Rejecting Torah Leads to Error and Division

When Marcion rejected the written Torah, he rejected everything connected to it.

- The God who gave it
- The prophets who preached it
- The Messiah who fulfilled it
- The apostles who taught it

This produced a fractured Gospel and a divided God. The same errors still spread today:

- Torah was abolished

THE RISE OF MARCION AND THE FALL OF THE FAITHFUL

- Torah is only for Jews
- Torah contradicts grace
- Torah is bondage

Scripture refutes each one of these.

"Torah was abolished."

Matthew 5:17 to 19 (NLT)
Not even the smallest detail of God's law will disappear.

Romans 3:31 (NKJV)
We establish the law through faith.

"Torah is only for Jews."

Acts 15:21 (NLT)
Gentiles were expected to hear Moses read every Sabbath.

Romans 11:17 (NLT)
Gentiles are grafted into the same olive tree.

"Torah contradicts grace."

Romans 6:14 to 15 (NLT)
Grace does not allow sin. Grace empowers obedience.

James 2:17 to 18 (NLT)
Faith without works is dead.

THE RISE OF MARCION AND THE FALL OF THE FAITHFUL

"Torah is bondage."

Psalm 119:45 (NLT)
"I will walk in freedom, for I have devoted myself to your commandments."

James 1:25 (NLT)
The perfect law sets you free.

John 14:15 (NLT)
"If you love me, obey my commandments."

Conclusion Torah Is Covenant Wisdom for the Redeemed

Torah never saved anyone. It never could. It was never designed to. It guides those whom God has already redeemed. Yeshua upheld it. Paul loved it. James taught it. The prophets rejoiced in it. The early believers lived it.

Torah and grace stand together, pointing to the same God and the same Messiah. Marcion rejected Torah because he misunderstood grace. The Scriptures show the truth. The Torah reveals the character of Yehovah. Yeshua is the living expression of that revelation.

THE RISE OF MARCION AND THE FALL OF THE FAITHFUL

Chapter 21 Denying the Hebrew Roots of the Gospel

Another major error that shaped Marcion's theology was the belief that the Gospel is a new Gentile religion that stands apart from Israel. He taught that the teachings of Moses and the prophets were irrelevant for believers, that the God of Israel was not the Father of Yeshua, and that the apostles abandoned their Jewish identity when they followed the Messiah. This was not a minor disagreement. It was a direct attack on the foundation of the Gospel itself.

Scripture presents the opposite. Every part of the Gospel is rooted in the Hebrew Scriptures. Every promise fulfilled in Yeshua came through the covenant God made with Abraham, Isaac, and Jacob. Every apostle lived within a Jewish worldview. The early believers did not sever themselves from Israel. They understood themselves as the continuation of God's work in Israel through the Messiah.

To disconnect the Gospel from its Hebrew roots is to misunderstand the Gospel entirely.

Yeshua and the Gospel Begin Within Israel

The New Testament begins by anchoring Yeshua inside the story of Israel.

Matthew 1:1 (NLT):
"This is a record of the ancestors of Jesus the Messiah, a descendant of David and of Abraham."

THE RISE OF MARCION AND THE FALL OF THE FAITHFUL

The Messiah does not arrive from outside. He comes as the promised son of Abraham and David.

Yeshua said:

John 4:22 (NLT):
"Salvation comes through the Jews."

He identifies the source of the Gospel. He affirms that God worked through Israel to bring salvation to the world.

Paul echoes this same truth.

Romans 9:4 to 5 (NLT):
"They are the people of Israel, chosen to be God's adopted children. God revealed his glory to them. He gave them the covenants and the law and the privilege of worshiping him and receiving his wonderful promises. Christ himself was an Israelite as far as his human nature is concerned."

The Gospel stands on Israel's story. It does not replace it.

The Apostles Remained Faithful Jews

Marcion claimed the apostles abandoned Jewish identity when they followed Yeshua. The New Testament shows the opposite.

Acts 3:1 (NLT):
"Peter and John went to the Temple one afternoon to take part in the three o'clock prayer service."
Approximate date: AD 30 to 32
Peter and John continued the standard Jewish prayer schedule in the Temple shortly after Yeshua's resurrection and ascension.

They continued daily Jewish prayer.

THE RISE OF MARCION AND THE FALL OF THE FAITHFUL

Acts 20:16 (NLT):
"Paul was eager to get to Jerusalem, if possible, in time for the Festival of Pentecost."
Approximate date: AD 55 to 57
More than twenty years after coming to faith in Yeshua, Paul still arranged his travels around the biblical festivals.

Paul kept the appointed times.

Acts 21:20 (NLT):
"You see, brother, how many thousands of Jews have also believed, and they all follow the law of Moses very seriously."
Approximate date: AD 57
This is Paul's final visit to Jerusalem before his arrest. The entire Jerusalem believing community was still Torah faithful decades after Pentecost.

The entire Jerusalem community remained committed to Torah.

The apostles did not create a new religion. They proclaimed the fulfillment of Israel's hope in Yeshua.

The Gospel Fulfilled What the Hebrew Scriptures Promised

The apostles did not invent the Gospel. They preached what the prophets promised long before Yeshua was born.

Luke 24:27 (NLT):
"Then Jesus took them through the writings of Moses and all the prophets, explaining from all the Scriptures the things concerning himself."

THE RISE OF MARCION AND THE FALL OF THE FAITHFUL

The Gospel is rooted in Moses and the prophets. It fulfills what they foretold.

Acts 10:43 (NLT):
"He is the one all the prophets testified about, saying that everyone who believes in him will have their sins forgiven through his name."

Peter does not quote new ideas. He quotes Scripture that Israel had preserved for centuries.

Acts 26:22 to 23 (NLT):
"I teach nothing except what the prophets and Moses said would happen. The Messiah would suffer and be the first to rise from the dead."

The Gospel is the continuation of Israel's story, not a replacement for it.

The First Believers Saw Themselves as Israel Renewed

The earliest name for the followers of Yeshua was not Christians. It was The Way, a name drawn from Torah and the prophets.

Acts 24:14 (NLT):
"I follow the Way, which they call a cult. I worship the God of our ancestors, and I firmly believe the Jewish law and everything written in the prophets."

Paul understood himself as part of Israel. He never saw himself outside of it.

Gentile believers were grafted into the covenant God made with Israel.

THE RISE OF MARCION AND THE FALL OF THE FAITHFUL

Romans 11:17 (NLT):
"You Gentiles have been grafted in. So now you also receive the blessing God has promised to Abraham and his children."

The Gospel does not create two peoples. It creates one family in the Messiah.

The Early Church Fathers Refuted Marcion on This Point

Writers such as Justin Martyr, Irenaeus, Tertullian, and Epiphanius all rejected the idea of a Gentile only Christianity. Their writings demonstrate complete agreement on several points.

- The God of Israel is the Father of Yeshua
- The Hebrew Scriptures point to the Messiah
- The apostles remained rooted in the Jewish way of life
- The Gospel fulfills the prophetic promises

Their work exposes Marcion's attempt to build a new religion without Israel.

Why This Matters for Us Today

Marcion's error continues to influence modern theology. Many believers unknowingly repeat ideas that started with him.

- The Old Testament is less important
- The Hebrew Scriptures were replaced by the New Testament
- The law was abolished at the cross
- The Jewish context is optional

THE RISE OF MARCION AND THE FALL OF THE FAITHFUL

- The Gospel is a Gentile religion

Each of these beliefs originated from Marcion.
They did not come from Yeshua. They did not come from the apostles. They did not come from the prophets. They arose from a second century teacher who attempted to separate the Gospel from its Hebrew foundation.

Each of these beliefs distorts the Gospel.

The Gospel does not erase Israel.
The Gospel fulfills the promises given to Israel.
The Gospel extends Israel's covenant blessing to the nations.
The Gospel reveals Yeshua as the promised Messiah of Israel who Invites the world into the same covenant.

To deny the Hebrew roots of the Gospel is to deny the story God told from the beginning.

Supporting Citations From Early Sources

The following primary source references support the historical claims made in this section about the Hebrew roots of the Gospel, the Jewish identity of the apostles, and the early Church's rejection of Marcion's teachings.

Justin Martyr

Dialogue with Trypho, Chapters 11, 18, 29, 47
Justin argues that the followers of Yeshua worship the God of Israel and accept the Hebrew Scriptures as authoritative.
He connects the Gospel directly to the prophets and to the covenant made with Abraham.

THE RISE OF MARCION AND THE FALL OF THE FAITHFUL

Irenaeus

Against Heresies, Book 3, Chapters 5 to 12
Irenaeus defends the unity between the God of Israel and the Father of Yeshua.
He refutes Marcion by showing that the apostles taught the fulfillment of the Law and the Prophets.

Against Heresies, Book 1, Chapters 26 to 27
Irenaeus describes Marcion's attempt to sever the Gospel from the Hebrew Scriptures and exposes it as a departure from apostolic teaching.

Tertullian

Against Marcion, Books 1 to 5
Tertullian gives a detailed rebuttal of Marcion's claims.
He shows that the apostles honored the Scriptures of Israel and taught continuity from Moses to the Messiah.
He argues that the Gospel cannot be understood apart from the Hebrew Bible.

Epiphanius

Panarion, Section 42 (Marcionites)
Epiphanius provides historical descriptions of Marcion's teachings and documents how the early Church condemned his rejection of the Hebrew Scriptures.

Eusebius

Ecclesiastical History, Books 2 and 3
Eusebius records that the earliest believers continued Jewish practices, participated in Temple life until its destruction, and understood themselves as the continuation of the Israelite faith.

THE RISE OF MARCION AND THE FALL OF THE FAITHFUL

The Didache

The Didache, Chapters 1 to 6
This early first century manual reflects strong continuity with Torah ethics and lifestyle.
It shows that the earliest followers of Yeshua practiced a form of Judaism centered on the Messiah.

Flavius Josephus

Antiquities of the Jews, Book 20
Josephus confirms that first century Jewish life remained centered on Torah, festivals, and Temple worship during the time when the apostles were active.

The Dead Sea Scrolls

These scrolls show how Jewish groups of the time understood covenant, law, purity, festivals, and Scripture.
They provide essential context for understanding the world in which Yeshua and the apostles lived and taught.

Chapter 22 Attacks on Gospel Authorship

Few attacks on the faith have been as persistent or as destructive as the claim that Matthew, Mark, Luke, and John did not write the Gospels that bear their names. These claims did not begin with modern scholars. They began with heretics. Marcion, the Gnostics, and later critics sought to break the link between the apostles and the written accounts of Yeshua's life. If the eyewitnesses can be removed, the Scriptures lose authority, the teachings lose weight, and the Gospel becomes open to reinvention.

The early believers rejected every attempt to sever authorship from the apostles. They preserved the testimony of those who knew the apostles personally. They passed down their statements with clarity, consistency, and remarkable unity.

The historical evidence is overwhelming. The internal evidence is compelling. The early church testimony is unanimous. The Gospels are apostolic.

Part 1 Just Tell Me What You Saw

Section 1 Eyewitness Intent, Eyewitness Claims, Eyewitness Sources

Before examining the external records, it is essential to recognize what the Gospels themselves claim.

Luke's Preface Shows a Direct Line to Eyewitnesses

THE RISE OF MARCION AND THE FALL OF THE FAITHFUL

Luke 1:1 to 4 (NLT):
"Many people have set out to write accounts about the events that have been fulfilled among us. They used the eyewitness reports circulating among us from the early disciples. Having carefully investigated everything from the beginning, I also have decided to write a careful account..."

Luke states plainly:

- He relied on eyewitnesses
- He investigated carefully
- He produced a historical account
- His purpose was certainty

This is the language of a historian, not a theologian inventing stories.

Cited by:
Eusebius, Ecclesiastical History 3.4.7
Irenaeus, Against Heresies 3.1.1
Origen, Commentary on John 1.6

John's Gospel Claims Eyewitness Testimony

John 19:35 (NLT):
"This report is from an eyewitness giving an accurate account. He speaks the truth so that you also may continue to believe."

John 21:24 (NLT):
"This disciple is the one who testifies to these events and has recorded them here."

THE RISE OF MARCION AND THE FALL OF THE FAITHFUL

John explicitly claims:

- He saw these events
- He recorded them
- His testimony is reliable

Cited by:
Irenaeus, Against Heresies 3.1.2
Clement of Alexandria, Fragments 39
Tertullian, Against Marcion 4.2

Internal Evidence for Matthew

Matthew contains:

- Jewish structure
- Heavy Torah emphasis
- Extensive use of Hebrew idioms
- A tax collector's economic precision
- Exact coin terms such as two-drachma and stater
- Direct knowledge of Galilee, Judea, and the Temple tax

No anonymous Gentile writer in the second century would know these details.

Cited by:
Papias, quoted in Eusebius, Ecclesiastical History 3.39.16
Irenaeus, Against Heresies 3.1.1
Origen, Commentary on Matthew 1.1

THE RISE OF MARCION AND THE FALL OF THE FAITHFUL

Section 2 Early Church Testimony A Unified, Unbroken Chain

This is where the case becomes overwhelming.

All early Christian witnesses agree on the authorship of the four Gospels.
There is complete unity across geography, language, culture, and theological perspective.
This unanimity is unmatched for any ancient biography.

Below are the most important citations, with approximate dates.

Papias of Hierapolis AD 95 to 120

Papias is the earliest named source after the apostles. He was a hearer of John and a companion of Polycarp.

Papias on Matthew

Papias, quoted in Eusebius, Ecclesiastical History 3.39.16:
"Matthew recorded the sayings in the Hebrew language, and each interpreted them as he was able."

This is the oldest external testimony to Matthew's authorship.

Papias on Mark

Eusebius, Ecclesiastical History 3.39.15:
"Mark, having become the interpreter of Peter, wrote down accurately everything he remembered. He made no mistake. He wrote with care what he remembered from Peter's teachings."

THE RISE OF MARCION AND THE FALL OF THE FAITHFUL

This testimony places Mark as Peter's companion and confirms Mark's Gospel as apostolic preaching in written form.

Papias carried immense authority in the early Church.

Justin Martyr AD 150 to 165

Justin refers to the Gospels as "the Memoirs of the Apostles."

Justin, First Apology 66:
"The apostles in the memoirs composed by them, which are called Gospels..."

Justin quotes material from Matthew, Mark, and Luke and attributes them to the apostles or apostolic companions.

Irenaeus of Lyons AD 175 to 190

Irenaeus was taught by Polycarp, who was taught by the apostle John.

Irenaeus gives the first full list of the four Gospels by name.

Irenaeus, Against Heresies 3.1.1:
"Matthew also issued a written Gospel among the Hebrews in their own dialect.
Mark, the disciple and interpreter of Peter, also handed down to us in writing what Peter had preached.
Luke, the companion of Paul, recorded the Gospel that Paul preached.
John, the disciple of the Lord, who also leaned on His breast, produced his Gospel while residing at Ephesus."

THE RISE OF MARCION AND THE FALL OF THE FAITHFUL

This testimony is direct, authoritative, and rooted in apostolic lineage.

The Muratorian Fragment AD 170 to 200

The earliest known canon list.

It confirms:

- Luke wrote Luke
- John wrote John
- Mark interpreted Peter
- Matthew was the first Gospel written

Tertullian AD 200 to 220

Tertullian aggressively refuted Marcion by appealing to Gospel authorship.

Tertullian, Against Marcion 4.2:
"We affirm that the Gospels are the work of the apostles, or of men who followed the apostles."

He names:

- Matthew the apostle
- John the apostle
- Mark the interpreter of Peter
- Luke the companion of Paul

THE RISE OF MARCION AND THE FALL OF THE FAITHFUL

Origen AD 230

Origen, Commentary on Matthew 1.1:
"Among the four Gospels, which are the only indisputable ones in the Church of God...
First is written according to Matthew...
Second according to Mark...
Third according to Luke...
Last according to John."

Origen's list is identical to Irenaeus's list written almost a century earlier.

Eusebius of Caesarea AD 315 to 325

Eusebius acts as a compiler of earlier sources.

Eusebius, Ecclesiastical History 3.24 to 3.39:
He records the unanimous tradition that Matthew, Mark, Luke, and John wrote the four Gospels.

There is no competing authorship tradition anywhere in the ancient world.

Section 3 The Silence of Counterclaims

Modern scholars often claim that the Gospels were written by unknown communities or anonymous editors. The ancient world never made such claims. There is:

- No early writer who attributes the Gospels to anyone else

THE RISE OF MARCION AND THE FALL OF THE FAITHFUL

- No rival authorship tradition
- No ancient dispute over the fourfold authorship
- No alternative names, communities, or editors

This silence is powerful evidence.
In ancient biography, competing claims show up quickly. For the Gospels, there are none.

Even heretics like Marcion accepted Luke as written by Luke. He rejected passages, but never authorship.

The Power of the Unbroken Witness

The complete absence of competing claims in the ancient world is not a small detail. It is one of the strongest confirmations of Gospel authorship we possess. In antiquity, biographies were often disputed. Philosophers, poets, and historians regularly had texts falsely attributed to them, and rival schools preserved more than one tradition when disagreements arose. The early Church, however, shows no tension regarding the Gospels. No letters. No debates. No alternative names. No competing theories. The closer we get to the apostles, the stronger and more unanimous the testimony becomes.

This speaks to a historical memory that was clear, public, and universally accepted. The men who heard the apostles preach and saw them minister were still alive when the Gospels circulated. Communities that received these writings knew who sent them. Churches guarded them. Elders quoted them. Heretics tried to twist their meaning, but they never challenged their authorship. If they could have discredited the origins of the Gospels, they would have tried, yet not one attempted it. This silence is a loud witness.

Every modern theory that assigns anonymous communities, late editors, or literary constructs to the Gospels contradicts the entire body of ancient testimony. It overturns the clear statements of Papias, Irenaeus, Justin, Tertullian, Origen, Clement, and Eusebius. It also contradicts the assumptions of heretical groups who had every incentive to attack authorship and yet did not. These modern theories collapse under the reality that no one in the first three centuries of the Church attributed the Gospels to anyone other than Matthew, Mark, Luke, and John.

This unanimity points to one conclusion. The Gospels were known, from the beginning, to be the work of the apostles and their close companions. They carried apostolic authority because they were written by apostolic hands or preserved apostolic testimony. To deny their authorship today is to reject the unbroken witness of early Christianity and elevate speculation over historical fact. The early believers preserved the truth with care, reverence, and precision. They knew exactly whose voices they were hearing when they opened the Gospels, and so can we.

Part 2 Systematic Refutation of Modern Critical Attacks

Section 1 Refuting the Claim of Anonymous Manuscripts

One of the most common modern assertions is that the Gospels were originally anonymous. Critics argue that because the earliest surviving fragments do not contain internal titles, the names Matthew, Mark, Luke, and John must have been added later. This claim collapses under every line of historical evidence. Manuscript evidence, ancient testimony, and historical logic all demonstrate that the Gospels bore their traditional authorship from the beginning.

---

1. *Every surviving Gospel manuscript with titles contains the traditional names*

Whenever titles appear in Gospel manuscripts, the titles are always the same:

- According to Matthew
- According to Mark
- According to Luke
- According to John

There are no manuscripts with titles such as:

- According to Peter
- According to Thomas
- According to an unknown elder
- According to the community of Antioch

Not one manuscript anywhere in the world contains an alternative authorship for any Gospel.

Major early manuscript witnesses include:

Codex Vaticanus AD 300s
Contains all four Gospels with traditional titles.

Codex Sinaiticus AD 300s
Contains the full New Testament with standard Gospel titles.

Codex Alexandrinus AD 400s
Contains the four Gospels with traditional titles.

Codex Bezae AD 400s
Contains the four Gospels and Acts with the usual titles.

Papyrus 66 AD 200
Contains most of the Gospel of John with the title According to John.

Papyrus 75 AD 200
Contains large portions of Luke and John with traditional titles.

There is no competing manuscript tradition.

---

2. Textus Receptus witnesses also preserve the same titles

The Byzantine manuscripts forming the foundation of the Textus Receptus match the Alexandrian witnesses completely. Not a single manuscript used by Erasmus, Stephanus, Beza, or the Elzevirs contains any alternative Gospel authorship.

Major Byzantine manuscripts include:

Codex Alexandrinus AD 400s
Bridges Alexandrian and Byzantine traditions. Preserves traditional titles.

Codex Cyprius K or 017 AD 900s
Contains all four Gospels with traditional titles.

Codex Campianus M or 021 AD 900s
Complete Byzantine Gospel codex with traditional titles.

Codex Petropolitanus Purpureus N or 022 AD 500s
Fragmentary but includes title sections with traditional authorship.

Codex Koridethi Θ or 038 AD 800s
Contains all four Gospels with standard titles.

Codex Basilensis E or 07 AD 800s
Used by Erasmus when forming the TR. Carries traditional titles.

Later Byzantine manuscripts used directly in the TR tradition:

Minuscule 1 AD 1100s
Used directly by Erasmus. Carries the traditional titles.

Minuscule 2 AD 1100s
Preserves traditional Gospel titles.

Minuscule 2814 AD 1100s
Contains Revelation. Gospel titles remain standard.

Minuscules 4, 5, 6, 35, 69, 330
All preserve the traditional titles.

The TR tradition matches the earliest papyri and earliest codices. Across every textual family and every century, the authorship is the same.

---

3. Ancient books rarely placed titles inside the main text

The earliest fragments of many ancient works do not contain internal titles. This was normal for scroll culture. Titles were usually written:

THE RISE OF MARCION AND THE FALL OF THE FAITHFUL

- On the outside of the scroll
- On a tag called a sillybos or index
- At the end of the work
- In library catalogs
- In church and synagogue inventories

Because of this, early fragments of many well-known works appear without internal titles. Yet no historian argues these works were anonymous.

Examples from Classical Literature

Herodotus, Histories
Earliest fragments such as P. Oxy. 2099 from the AD 100s lack internal titles.
Herodotus is universally affirmed as the author.

Thucydides, History of the Peloponnesian War
Fragments such as P. Oxy. 16 from the AD 100s contain no internal title.
Authorship is uncontested.

Euripides, Hippolytus
P. Oxy. 852 from AD 100 to 150 contains the text but no title.
No scholar questions Euripides' authorship.

Sophocles, Oedipus Tyrannus
Papyri such as P. Vindob. 29780 lack titles.
Sophocles remains the accepted author.

Homer, Iliad and Odyssey
Early papyri such as P. Oxy. 20, 221, and 421 lack titles and book

THE RISE OF MARCION AND THE FALL OF THE FAITHFUL

divisions.
Homer remains the uncontested author.

Examples from Jewish and Greco Roman Historians

Josephus, Antiquities of the Jews
Fragments such as P. Vindob. G 39777 from AD 100s to 200s lack internal titles.
Josephus remains the uncontested author.

Philo of Alexandria
Numerous treatises survive in fragments without titles.
Authorship is universally agreed upon.

Tacitus, Histories
Early medieval copies lack formal title pages.
Tacitus remains the uncontested author.

Polybius, Histories
Fragments such as P. Oxy. 1364 from the AD 100s contain the text but no title.
His authorship is undisputed.

Examples from Early Christian Writings Outside the NT

1 Clement AD 96
Earliest copies lack an internal title.
Early church testimony unanimously attributes it to Clement.

The Shepherd of Hermas AD 100 to 150
Early papyri lack internal titles.
Still attributed correctly through early church tradition.

The Didache AD 50 to 100
Survives without a title page.
Early Christians identified it without confusion.

What This Shows

The absence of internal titles in the earliest Gospel fragments is:

- Normal for antiquity
- Common across multiple genres
- Not evidence of anonymity
- Not evidence of later additions

No historian argues Herodotus, Tacitus, Josephus, Homer, or Sophocles were anonymous because their earliest fragments lack internal titles.

Applying this standard only to the Gospels is inconsistent.

4. The Gospels circulated as a four fold collection by the mid second century

Before AD 170 the four Gospels were already grouped together and treated as a unified authoritative collection.

Theophilus of Antioch AD 168
Quotes all four Gospels as Scripture.

The Muratorian Fragment AD 170 to 200
Lists all four Gospels by name and rejects alternatives.

THE RISE OF MARCION AND THE FALL OF THE FAITHFUL

A collection cannot exist without known authors.
If the Gospels were anonymous, we would see:

- Regional disagreements
- Competing names
- Uncertain attributions
- Confusion

But early Christianity presents a united testimony.

5. *Anonymous works never produce universal, uncontested attribution*

Truly anonymous works in antiquity always produced competing authorship claims. This consistent pattern appears across pagan, Jewish, and Christian literature.

Here are the clearest examples.

The Epistle to the Hebrews

Competing authors:

- Paul
  (Clement of Alexandria, Eastern churches)
- Barnabas
  (Tertullian explicitly attributes Hebrews to Barnabas)
- Luke
  (Origen suggests Luke translated a Hebrew sermon of Paul)

- Apollos
  (Martin Luther and many modern scholars)
- Clement of Rome
  (some early Latin traditions)
- Priscilla
  (Hypothesized by Adolf Harnack in modern scholarship)

There is no unified ancient tradition.

The Shepherd of Hermas

Competing authors:

- Hermas, brother of Pius I
- A prophet named Hermas
- An unknown visionary

Three different theories.

The Apocalypse of Peter

Competing authors:

- The apostle Peter
- A pseudonymous writer
- An Egyptian visionary

No single accepted view.

The Gospel of Thomas

Competing authors:

- Didymus Judas Thomas
- A Syrian Gnostic community
- A Valentinian compiler
- Edessa traditions

Multiple conflicting claims.

The Gospel of the Hebrews

Competing authors:

- Matthew in Hebrew
- An unknown Nazarene
- A Jewish Christian elder

All contradictory.

The Gospel of the Egyptians

Competing authors:

- A Gnostic writer
- A second century syncretist

No unified claim.

THE RISE OF MARCION AND THE FALL OF THE FAITHFUL

The Gospel of Peter

Competing authors:

- The apostle Peter
- A docetic writer
- An unknown visionary

No consensus.

The Pattern in Every Case

Anonymous or pseudonymous books always generate:

- competing names
- contradictory traditions
- regional variations
- debates in early church lists

This is how anonymity functions in antiquity.

But for the Four Gospels?

There is not a single alternative author in any ancient source for:

- Matthew
- Mark
- Luke
- John

THE RISE OF MARCION AND THE FALL OF THE FAITHFUL

No disagreements.
No competing claims.
No regional variations.
No anonymous theories.
No controversy.

The universal agreement across all regions of the early Church is historically impossible unless the authorship was known from the beginning.

---

6. The early church lived close enough to the apostles to know the truth

The earliest believers were taught directly by the apostles and their disciples. They passed down long lists of bishops and church leaders. They preserved their Scriptures with careful guardianship.

They did not misplace the authorship of their most treasured books.

---

7. Testimony from Papias destroys the anonymous manuscript argument

Papias lived in the generation after the apostles. He personally knew men taught by John.

He reports:

- Matthew wrote his Gospel
- Mark wrote down Peter's teachings

His record dates to AD 95 to 120.
No critic has any evidence earlier than Papias.

8. Even the enemies of Christianity never denied Gospel authorship

Pagan and heretical critics attacked miracles, morals, prophecy, the character of believers, and the claims of Yeshua.
Yet none of them ever claimed:

- The Gospels were anonymous
- The Gospels were falsely attributed
- The early church erred in naming the authors

Enemies of the faith attacked everything else, but not authorship.

Examples:

Celsus AD 170
Rejected Christian doctrine but never denied Gospel authorship.

Porphyry AD 270
Rejected Christian prophecy but never claimed the Gospels were anonymous.

Their silence is powerful.

Conclusion to Section 1

The idea that the Gospels were originally anonymous is:

- Unsupported by manuscripts
- Contradicted by every textual family

THE RISE OF MARCION AND THE FALL OF THE FAITHFUL

- Refuted by the TR and Byzantine witnesses
- Disproven by ancient literary practice
- Rejected by early church testimony
- Ignored by ancient critics
- Historically implausible

Across all manuscript traditions, all centuries, and all regions, the Gospels have always carried the names of Matthew, Mark, Luke, and John.

There is no evidence of anonymity.
There is no evidence of alternate authors.
There is no evidence of later additions.

The traditional authorship is the only historically defensible conclusion.

The only historical exception comes from Marcion, who produced a mutilated version of Luke's Gospel in the second century. Marcion removed the birth narratives, the prophecies, the Old Testament quotations, the teachings he disliked, and every reference to the God of Israel. He then renamed his edited version The Gospel of the Lord. Yet even Marcion did not deny that the original work was written by Luke. His actions show that he accepted Luke's authorship and simply cut out what contradicted his theology. The fact that the earliest heretic to alter a Gospel still affirmed its author only strengthens the universal tradition that the Gospels were known from the beginning by the names Matthew, Mark, Luke, and John.

THE RISE OF MARCION AND THE FALL OF THE FAITHFUL

Section 2 Refuting the Q Source Theory

The Q Source Theory claims that Matthew and Luke copied large portions of their Gospels from a lost, hypothetical document scholars call Q. This theory was created to explain the similarities between Matthew and Luke, especially where they agree against Mark. But Q has never been found. No church father mentions it. No manuscript contains it. No ancient writer lists it. Q is entirely theoretical and exists only on paper.

When examined historically, linguistically, and logically, the Q theory collapses. Every major line of evidence refutes it.

---

1. No ancient writer ever mentions a document like Q

Every major early Christian writer who discusses the Gospels, manuscripts, apostolic traditions, or church libraries is completely silent on any sayings source, lost Gospel, or shared document used by Matthew and Luke.

Writers who never mention Q include:

Papias AD 95 to 120
Justin Martyr AD 150
Irenaeus AD 175
Clement of Alexandria AD 180
Tertullian AD 200
Origen AD 230
Hippolytus AD 200
Eusebius AD 315
Epiphanius AD 350
Jerome AD 380
Augustine AD 400

THE RISE OF MARCION AND THE FALL OF THE FAITHFUL

These men discussed:

- Matthew's authorship
- Mark's connection to Peter
- Luke's investigative method
- John's eyewitness role
- Canon lists
- Lost books
- False gospels
- Church archives

Yet not one of them hints at a Q document.
The silence is total.

---

2. Q is unnecessary because Luke explains his own sources

Luke tells us exactly how he compiled his Gospel.

Luke 1:1 to 4 NLT:
"Many people have set out to write accounts... They used the eyewitness reports circulating among us... Having carefully investigated everything from the beginning, I also have decided to write a careful account..."

Luke explicitly states:

- He used written accounts
- He used eyewitness testimony

THE RISE OF MARCION AND THE FALL OF THE FAITHFUL

- He conducted personal investigation
- He wrote with precision

There is no hint of a secret sayings source.
Luke already tells us what he used.

3. Matthew and Luke agree because they follow the same Teacher

The simplest reason Matthew and Luke share material is because they recorded the teachings of the same Person. Two disciples writing down the words of Yeshua at different times will naturally produce:

- identical sayings
- similar phrasing
- matching parables
- parallel teachings

This is normal for ancient biography. No historian invents hypothetical sources when two students of a teacher record the same instruction.

4. Q requires Matthew and Luke to be independent, which is historically impossible

Q theorists assume Matthew and Luke never saw each other's work. But history contradicts this assumption.

Early church testimony confirms:

THE RISE OF MARCION AND THE FALL OF THE FAITHFUL

- Matthew wrote first
- Mark wrote Peter's preaching
- Luke wrote after investigating everything
- Luke knew Paul
- Luke likely spent time in the Holy Land
- Luke wrote after many accounts were circulating

Luke had access to Matthew.
The idea that Luke wrote a Gospel without ever seeing Matthew is historically unrealistic.

---

5. Q requires Matthew to avoid Luke, and Luke to avoid Matthew

If Matthew and Luke used Q without knowing each other's Gospels, both must have independently:

- copied Q
- added unique material
- avoided each other's additions
- structured their events differently
- yet created overlapping teachings with identical wording

This level of coincidence has no parallel in ancient literature.

THE RISE OF MARCION AND THE FALL OF THE FAITHFUL

6. Q contradicts the unanimous testimony of the early church

Every ancient writer who comments on Gospel origins affirms:

- Matthew wrote first
- Luke used earlier accounts
- The Gospels came from apostles and their companions

Papias, Irenaeus, Origen, and Jerome all affirm a direct apostolic line. They never mention a lost sayings Gospel and never hint at a shared literary source.

Q contradicts the entire historical record.

---

7. No manuscript of Q has ever been found

There is no:

- scrap
- fragment
- quote
- catalog entry
- early reference
- mention in canon debates
- copy in any ancient library
- reference by any church father
- reference by any heretic

THE RISE OF MARCION AND THE FALL OF THE FAITHFUL

Every major pseudepigraphal gospel is mentioned somewhere by someone:

- Gospel of Thomas
- Gospel of Peter
- Gospel of the Hebrews
- Gospel of the Egyptians
- Protoevangelium of James

But Q is never mentioned. Not one time.

A major sayings source used by Matthew and Luke would not disappear without trace while dozens of fringe gospels survived.

---

8. Q violates Occam's Razor

The simplest explanation for why Matthew and Luke share material is that they recorded the teachings of the same Person and drew from the same historical events.

This is where Occam's Razor applies. Occam's Razor states that the explanation with the fewest assumptions is most likely to be correct. When two theories explain the same data, the simpler one should be preferred.

Simple explanation:

Matthew and Luke share material because:

- They followed the same Teacher
- Yeshua repeated core teachings in many settings

THE RISE OF MARCION AND THE FALL OF THE FAITHFUL

- Early believers preserved sayings through oral and written tradition
- Luke used written accounts he mentions in his preface

This explanation fits all known historical data.

Q's explanation:

Matthew and Luke share material because:

- A lost sayings document once existed
- It circulated widely
- Both Matthew and Luke used it
- They avoided using each other
- It left no manuscript copies
- It left no quotations
- It left no references
- No church father mentioned it
- No heretic mentioned it
- No early catalog listed it
- It disappeared without any trace
- Every early Christian forgot it existed

Q requires far more assumptions than the simple historical explanation.
Occam's Razor rejects Q.

THE RISE OF MARCION AND THE FALL OF THE FAITHFUL

9. The double tradition is explained by normal oral and written transmission

The material shared by Matthew and Luke, often called the double tradition, is consistent with:

- shared oral teachings
- synagogue teaching patterns
- repeated sayings used by Yeshua
- early written notes known as hypomnemata
- early catechetical summaries
- traveling disciples who preserved core material

No hypothetical document is needed.

10. Q collapses when Matthew and Luke's differences are examined

If Matthew and Luke copied the same document, one would expect similar structure and similar placement of shared sayings.

But Matthew and Luke:

- place the same sayings in different settings
- change audiences
- adjust order
- combine and separate material
- shape themes independently

THE RISE OF MARCION AND THE FALL OF THE FAITHFUL

This shows they are not following a fixed document.

Conclusion to Section 2

The Q Source Theory is:

- unattested
- unmentioned
- unfound
- unnecessary
- historically implausible
- contradicted by early testimony
- contradicted by Luke's preface
- contradicted by manuscript evidence
- logically convoluted
- rejected by Occam's Razor

The similarities between Matthew and Luke are best explained by:

- shared eyewitness testimony
- shared oral traditions
- shared written accounts
- shared historical events
- shared teachings of Yeshua

THE RISE OF MARCION AND THE FALL OF THE FAITHFUL

No ancient historian needs a hypothetical lost document to explain why two disciples recorded the same Teacher.

THE RISE OF MARCION AND THE FALL OF THE FAITHFUL

Section 3 Refuting Literary Dependence Theories

Literary Dependence Theories argue that Matthew and Luke relied heavily on Mark's Gospel when writing their own accounts. The most common form is called Markan Priority, which claims that Mark wrote first and that Matthew and Luke copied most of Mark. This theory stands at the core of much modern critical scholarship.

But Markan Priority breaks down when examined historically, linguistically, and theologically. The evidence points not to literary dependence on Mark, but to a shared historical reality: the life and teachings of Yeshua, preserved by eyewitnesses and early disciples.

---

1. Markan Priority contradicts the unanimous testimony of the early church

Every early Christian writer who discusses the order of the Gospels teaches:

- Matthew wrote first
- Mark wrote Peter's preaching
- Luke wrote after careful investigation
- John wrote last

There is no ancient testimony supporting Markan Priority.

Key witnesses include:

THE RISE OF MARCION AND THE FALL OF THE FAITHFUL

Papias AD 95 to 120
Matthew first, Mark wrote Peter's teaching.

Irenaeus AD 175
Matthew first, then Mark after Peter's departure.

Clement of Alexandria AD 180
The Gospels with genealogies were written first, meaning Matthew and Luke.

Origen AD 230
Matthew, then Mark, then Luke, then John.

Jerome AD 380
Same order.

There is no ancient source that places Mark first.

---

2. Mark's rougher Greek argues for originality, not priority

Modern critics argue Mark wrote first because his Greek is more primitive. But in ancient biography, simpler language does not indicate priority. It often indicates:

- direct eyewitness recollection
- oral teaching style
- rapid recording of Peter's preaching
- shorter, action driven narrative

Mark reflects the voice of Peter, a fisherman, not a trained scribe.
Matthew, a tax collector, writes with more structure.
Luke, a historian, writes with higher Greek.
John writes in simple vocabulary but with deep theological clarity

THE RISE OF MARCION AND THE FALL OF THE FAITHFUL

shaped by decades of reflection as an eyewitness and elder. Differences reflect authors, not dependence.

3. Why Mark Reads Like Preaching, Not a Primary Source

If Mark had written the first Gospel and Matthew and Luke simply copied him, then we should expect their work to look like normal literary expansion. But when you compare the books side by side, that is not what you find. Mark reads nothing like a full biography. It reads exactly like what the early Church said it was: the preaching notes of Peter. His Gospel moves quickly, focuses on action, and offers short summaries of moments that later writers expand with fuller detail. It is the rhythm of an eyewitness telling a story, not the structure of an author building a biography.

Mark leaves out material no ancient biographer would ignore if he were writing the first account of Yeshua's life. There is no birth narrative, no genealogy, no Sermon on the Mount, no Lord's Prayer, no extended teachings, no Beatitudes, no fulfillment sections, and no resurrection appearances. If Mark wrote first, then both Matthew and Luke would have to take Mark's short, fast-paced collection of scenes and transform it into two full-length biographies that include birth stories, genealogical records, long sermons, dozens of parables, prophetic fulfillments, and entire resurrection chapters. There is nothing like that kind of expansion anywhere in ancient literature. Editors do not enlarge a brief preaching outline into two massive biographies while supposedly following that outline as a base. It simply does not happen.

Mark makes perfect sense when understood as the record of Peter's public preaching. His omissions reflect the priorities of a traveling

THE RISE OF MARCION AND THE FALL OF THE FAITHFUL

apostle who emphasized action, miracles, and urgency. Public preaching rarely includes long teaching blocks or genealogical detail. Listeners did not expect an infancy narrative. They needed to hear what Yeshua did and what He commanded them to do. Peter's style matches what we see in Mark: memory-driven storytelling, vivid detail, and short snapshots of teachings that Matthew and Luke later expand.

Matthew and Luke write very differently. They are building complete accounts. They draw from other eyewitness testimony, early written notes, repeated teachings Yeshua gave across villages, and their own careful investigation. Luke openly states this in his prologue. They do not behave like editors revising Mark. They behave like independent authors telling the full story from the sources available to them.

The real problem with Markan Priority is not deletion. It is the unrealistic expansion required. Matthew and Luke would have to take a short preaching outline and independently reshape it into two massive, richly structured biographies. At the same time, they would have to keep some of Mark's features, ignore others, rearrange his order freely, relocate sayings, expand teachings he barely mentions, and develop themes he does not treat. That is not how ancient editors worked. That is how independent authors using shared history and shared testimony write.

Mark reflects the voice of Peter preaching.
Matthew, Luke, and John reflect the voices of authors writing full biographies.

This is why the early Church never believed Mark wrote first.
The content, structure, and ancient testimony all point in the same direction.

THE RISE OF MARCION AND THE FALL OF THE FAITHFUL

4. Matthew and Luke include material that Mark does not know

If Matthew and Luke used Mark, they would not share large blocks of material that Mark never records.

Shared material outside Mark includes:

- infancy narratives
- genealogies
- Beatitudes
- the Lord's Prayer
- major teachings
- parables
- miracles unique to Matthew and Luke

This fits:

- independent eyewitness sources
- repeated public teaching by Yeshua
- early Jewish Christian written notes

Not copying Mark.

THE RISE OF MARCION AND THE FALL OF THE FAITHFUL

5. Matthew and Luke do not follow Mark's order

If Matthew and Luke copied Mark, they would follow Mark's structure. They do not.

Matthew rearranges material thematically.
Luke rearranges material narratively.
Both reorder entire sections.

Copyists do not behave like this.
Independent authors do.

---

6. Matthew uses far more Old Testament fulfillment material than Mark

If Matthew copied Mark, why would he add:

- dozens of Old Testament citations
- long sermons
- fulfillment formulas
- structured teaching blocks

Matthew's Gospel reflects original composition shaped for a Jewish audience. It does not read like an edited version of Mark.

---

7. Mark preserves Aramaic expressions that Matthew and Luke translate or omit

Mark contains Aramaic phrases such as:

- Talitha koum

THE RISE OF MARCION AND THE FALL OF THE FAITHFUL

- Eloi, Eloi, lama sabachthani
- Boanerges
- Ephphatha
- Corban

These point to:

- raw eyewitness memory
- Peter's preaching voice
- historical authenticity

Matthew and Luke adjust these phrases for their audiences. This is the behavior of independent authors, not editors of Mark.

8. Mark's vivid eyewitness details reflect Peter's perspective

Mark includes sensory and emotional detail such as:

- green grass at the feeding
- a pillow in the boat
- time markers
- gestures
- specific movements
- reactions and emotions

These features reflect eyewitness testimony.
If Matthew and Luke had copied Mark, they would not remove such

THE RISE OF MARCION AND THE FALL OF THE FAITHFUL

vivid detail.
They remove it because they are drawing from their own sources.

9. Mark's abrupt ending contradicts the idea that Matthew and Luke expanded him

Mark ends with the women fleeing from the tomb, with no resurrection appearance.

Matthew and Luke:

- add new resurrection scenes
- provide new teachings
- introduce new characters
- portray Yeshua in new settings

They do not follow Mark's structure or flow.
They write independent, fuller accounts.

10. Markan Priority requires Matthew and Luke to behave unnaturally

To accept Markan Priority, one must believe that Matthew and Luke:

- used Mark as their main source
- ignored large parts of Mark
- changed Mark's order freely
- removed eyewitness details

THE RISE OF MARCION AND THE FALL OF THE FAITHFUL

- added identical sayings independently
- created new scenes separately

This does not match the way ancient editors worked.

11. Markan Priority creates more problems than it solves

Markan Priority cannot explain:

- why early testimony never mentions Mark first
- why Matthew and Luke agree against Mark in many places
- why Matthew and Luke share material Mark does not have
- why Mark lacks essential teaching
- why Mark retains Aramaic phrases Matthew and Luke smooth out
- why Mark contains vivid detail Matthew and Luke omit

The theory raises more questions than it answers.

12. The simpler explanation is independent composition from shared apostolic tradition

The historical explanation is simple:

- Matthew wrote first
- Mark preserved Peter's preaching
- Luke investigated many accounts while eyewitnesses lived
- John wrote last as an aging eyewitness elder

THE RISE OF MARCION AND THE FALL OF THE FAITHFUL

This fits ancient testimony, manuscript evidence, and historical practice.

It also reflects the pattern of early Christian preaching and memory.

Conclusion to Section 3

Literary Dependence Theories, including Markan Priority, are:

- unsupported by ancient testimony
- contradicted by early church history
- inconsistent with manuscript evidence
- unable to explain major differences
- based on assumptions rather than historical reality
- contrary to ancient writing methods

The similarities between the synoptic Gospels arise from:

- shared historical events
- shared teachings
- shared eyewitness traditions
- shared early written sources
- shared apostolic preaching

Matthew, Mark, Luke, and John did not copy each other. They wrote as independent witnesses grounded in the same historical truth.

Dating Summary

The evidence presented in this appendix makes late dating theories impossible. If Matthew wrote first as every ancient source confirms, if Mark wrote from Peter's preaching before the apostle's death, if Luke investigated many eyewitness accounts while they were still living, and if John wrote last as an eyewitness elder near the end of the first century, then all four Gospels must be dated within the lifetime of the first generation of believers. Their content reflects living memory, not distant reconstruction. Their prophecy reflects revelation, not hindsight. Their historical detail reflects firsthand experience, not second century legend. The only dating model supported by manuscript evidence, early testimony, internal coherence, and historical reality is an early first century composition for the four Gospels.

In Conclusion

The claim that the Gospels were written by unknown editors or anonymous communities collapses under every line of evidence. The manuscripts preserve the same four names across every region and every century. The early church fathers, from Papias to Irenaeus to Origen and Eusebius, present a unified and unbroken testimony. Even heretics like Marcion, who rejected the content of Luke, still affirmed Luke as the author. The internal evidence matches the external record. Matthew writes like a Jewish disciple steeped in Torah. Mark records the preaching of Peter. Luke speaks with the voice of a trained historian who interviewed eyewitnesses. John writes as an aging witness who saw the events firsthand. Anonymous works always produce competing attributions. The Gospels produce none. No ancient writer ever suggests any other author. No competing names ever appear. No rival traditions ever

THE RISE OF MARCION AND THE FALL OF THE FAITHFUL

surface. The closer we move to the time of the apostles, the stronger the witness becomes. The early church lived close enough to the events to know the truth, and they guarded that truth with care. Modern theories of anonymous origins contradict the entire historical record and require us to ignore the testimony of those who received, copied, preached, and protected these writings from the beginning. The only historically defensible conclusion is the one the early believers always held. Matthew wrote Matthew. Mark wrote Mark. Luke wrote Luke. John wrote John.

THE RISE OF MARCION AND THE FALL OF THE FAITHFUL

Chapter 23 The False Divide Between Law and Grace

Section 1: The Scriptures Never Present Law and Grace as Opposites

Marcion taught that the Torah belonged to a harsh Old Testament deity and that grace came from a new and different god. A similar idea still lingers in many churches today. People assume that law and grace stand in opposition or that grace replaced the commandments. Scripture teaches the opposite. Law and grace work together. They come from the same God. They reveal the same character. They serve the same purpose in His covenant.

The Torah reveals the holiness of Yehovah and exposes sin. Grace forgives the sinner, cleanses the heart, and empowers obedience.
The two are not enemies. They work in unity.

To separate them is to repeat Marcion's error.

Yeshua affirms the Torah as eternal

Matthew 5:17 to 19 (NLT):
"Do not misunderstand why I have come. I did not come to abolish the law of Moses or the writings of the prophets. No, I came to accomplish their purpose. I tell you the truth, until heaven and earth disappear, not even the smallest detail of God's law will disappear until its purpose is achieved."

THE RISE OF MARCION AND THE FALL OF THE FAITHFUL

Heaven and earth remain.
The Torah remains.
Yeshua affirmed it, taught it, upheld it, and lived it.

Yeshua teaches that breaking the commandments leads to ruin

Matthew 7:26 to 27 (NLT):
"Anyone who hears My teaching and ignores it is foolish, like a person who builds a house on sand. When the rains and floods come and the winds beat against that house, it will collapse with a mighty crash."

Ignoring His teaching leads to destruction.
And Yeshua makes clear that His teaching is not separate from the Father.

John 7:16 (NLT):
"My message is not My own. It comes from God who sent Me."

Rejecting His words is rejecting the Father's words.
Disobedience is not covered by grace.
Disobedience destroys.

John says love for Yehovah is expressed through obedience

1 John 5:3 (NLT):
"Loving God means keeping His commandments, and His commandments are not burdensome."

John does not see obedience as bondage.
He sees it as love expressed.

Paul says faith establishes the Torah, not abolishes it

THE RISE OF MARCION AND THE FALL OF THE FAITHFUL

Romans 3:31 (NKJV):
"Do we then make void the law through faith? Certainly not. On the contrary, we establish the law."

Faith does not cancel Torah.
Faith confirms Torah.
Faith strengthens obedience.

Grace does not remove the commandments. Grace trains us to obey.

Titus 2:11 to 12 (NLT):
"For the grace of God has been revealed, bringing salvation to all people. And we are instructed to turn from godless living and sinful pleasures. We should live in this evil world with wisdom, righteousness, and devotion to God."

Grace does not erase standards.
Grace empowers holiness.

Paul teaches that the Spirit writes the Torah on the heart

Romans 8:3 to 4 (NLT):
"God declared an end to sin's control over us by giving His Son as a sacrifice for our sins. He did this so that the just requirement of the law would be fully satisfied for us, who no longer follow our sinful nature but instead follow the Spirit."

The Spirit empowers obedience.
The Spirit produces righteousness.
The Spirit fulfills the Torah within the believer.

James teaches that Torah is the Law of Freedom

James 1:25 (NLT):
"But if you look carefully into the perfect law that sets you free, and

if you do what it says and do not forget what you heard, then God will bless you for doing it."

Obedience and blessing remain linked.
Torah is freedom, not bondage.

Justification and sanctification must be kept distinct

Confusion about Torah often comes from mixing justification and sanctification. When believers call for obedience, critics accuse them of trying to earn salvation. This reveals a misunderstanding of how Scripture divides these two truths.

Justification is the free gift of Yehovah

Justification cannot be earned.
It is instant, complete, and based entirely on the finished work of Yeshua.

Romans 3:24 (NLT):
"Yet God, in His grace, freely makes us right in His sight."

Ephesians 2:8 to 9 (NLT):
"God saved you by His grace when you believed. And you cannot take credit for this."

Justification places a believer into covenant.

Sanctification is the fruit that grows after justification

Sanctification is the ongoing transformation produced by the Spirit.
It is the visible evidence of salvation.
It is the life of obedience that follows faith.

James 2:18 (NLT):
"How can you show me your faith if you don't have good deeds?"

THE RISE OF MARCION AND THE FALL OF THE FAITHFUL

A redeemed life produces obedience.
A tree is known by its fruit.

Obedience is the expression of love within covenant

John 14:15 (NLT):
"If you love Me, obey My commandments."

We do not obey to be saved.
We obey because we have been saved.
Justification is the root.
Sanctification is the fruit.

Obedience is not earning salvation. It is walking in sanctification.

Grace removes the penalty of sin.
Grace empowers us to walk in righteousness.
The Spirit writes the Torah on our hearts.
A redeemed people walk in the ways of their King.

Those who accuse Torah observance of being works salvation misunderstand the nature of covenant. Obedience is the result of salvation, not the cause of it. It is the fruit of love, the mark of discipleship, and the evidence of the Spirit at work.

We follow the Torah because we belong to Yeshua.
We obey because we love Him.
We keep His commandments because we are His.

Section 2: Grace Does Not Cancel Torah. Grace Empowers Obedience.

Marcion taught that grace replaced the commandments. Many modern teachers unknowingly repeat his ideas. They say grace

THE RISE OF MARCION AND THE FALL OF THE FAITHFUL

frees us from obedience or that the Torah contradicts the Gospel. Scripture presents a completely different picture. Grace does not erase Yehovah's instructions. Grace enables believers to walk in them with a renewed heart.

The false divide between law and grace is one of the most destructive inheritances from Marcion's influence.

Paul consistently connects grace to obedience

Paul uses the word grace more than any other biblical writer, yet he never presents grace as permission to ignore Yehovah's commandments. Paul presents grace as the power that transforms a believer so they can live in righteousness.

Romans 6:1 to 2 (NLT):
"Well then, should we keep on sinning so that God can show us more and more of His wonderful grace? Of course not. Since we have died to sin, how can we continue to live in it?"

Grace is not an excuse for sin.
Grace is the power to leave sin behind.

Romans 6:14 (NLT):
"Sin is no longer your master, for you no longer live under the requirements of the law. Instead, you live under the freedom of God's grace."

Sin loses its authority.
Grace sets a believer free to obey.

Romans 6:16 to 18 (NLT):
"You can be a slave to sin, which leads to death, or you can choose to obey God, which leads to righteous living."

THE RISE OF MARCION AND THE FALL OF THE FAITHFUL

Paul's teaching is simple and consistent.
Grace leads to obedience.
Grace does not replace it.

Grace trains believers to live by Yehovah's standards

Titus 2:11 to 12 (NLT):
"For the grace of God has been revealed, bringing salvation to all people. And we are instructed to turn from godless living and sinful pleasures."

Grace brings salvation.
Grace also brings instruction.

Grace teaches believers to turn from sin and walk in righteousness according to Yehovah's ways.

Grace fulfills the Torah's righteous requirement in us

Romans 8:3 to 4 (NLT):
"He did this so that the just requirement of the law would be fully satisfied for us, who no longer follow our sinful nature but instead follow the Spirit."

Paul does not say the Torah's righteous requirement is erased.
He says it is fulfilled in us.
Not abolished.
Accomplished by the Spirit.

The Spirit writes the Torah into the daily life of the believer.

Paul calls the Torah holy, just, and good

Romans 7:12 (NLT):
"But still, the law itself is holy, and its commands are holy and right and good."

THE RISE OF MARCION AND THE FALL OF THE FAITHFUL

Paul rejects any idea that Torah is a burden or a curse.
The Torah is holy.
Sin is the problem.

Romans 7:22 (NLT):
"I love God's law with all my heart."

A redeemed heart delights in Torah.

Grace removes condemnation, not obedience

Romans 8:1 (NLT):
"So now there is no condemnation for those who belong to Christ Jesus."

Condemnation is removed.
Judgment is removed.
Penalty is removed.

But obedience is not removed.

Romans 8:2 (NLT):
"And because you belong to Him, the power of the life-giving Spirit has freed you from the power of sin."

Grace frees us from slavery to sin so we can walk in righteousness. The Spirit frees us from disobedience, not from Yehovah's instructions.

Paul warns that lawlessness is the mark of deception

2 Thessalonians 2:7 to 8 (NLT):
"For this lawlessness is already at work secretly. The man of lawlessness will come, and the Lord Jesus will slay him with the breath of His mouth."

THE RISE OF MARCION AND THE FALL OF THE FAITHFUL

The spirit of lawlessness marks the end times.
Grace does not produce lawlessness.
Grace produces holiness.

Yeshua warns the same thing.

Matthew 24:12 (CJB):
"And many people's love will grow cold because of increased distance from Torah."

Love grows cold when Torah is abandoned.
Lawlessness destroys love.

Grace restores the purpose of Torah in the believer's life

Grace does not replace Torah.
Grace restores Torah to its proper place.

Torah never saved anyone.
It reveals Yehovah's character.
Grace restores believers so they can walk in that character.

Torah defines righteousness.
Grace empowers righteous living.

Torah shows what holiness looks like.
Grace shapes believers into a holy people.

Torah reveals sin.
Grace forgives sin and breaks its power.

The two work hand in hand in covenant.

Why this matters

The false divide between law and grace creates spiritual confusion.
It leads believers to think obedience is optional or even harmful.

But Scripture reveals that grace does not weaken Yehovah's standards. Grace strengthens the believer so the commandments can be lived out in love and faithfulness.

Grace does not cancel Torah.
Grace establishes Torah in the life of a redeemed person.

Section 3: The Torah Is Not Bondage. Sin Is Bondage.

One of the most damaging misconceptions in modern Christianity is the idea that Torah equals bondage. This belief comes directly from Marcion's influence. Scripture teaches the opposite. Torah is freedom. Sin is bondage. Torah is life. Sin is slavery. The commandments were never the problem. The sinful nature was the problem. Grace does not free believers from obedience. Grace frees believers from the power of sin so they can walk in obedience with joy.

Paul says slavery comes from sin, not from Torah

Romans 6:16 (NLT):
"You can be a slave to sin, which leads to death, or you can choose to obey God, which leads to righteous living."

Slavery comes from sin.
Freedom comes from obedience.

Paul never calls Yehovah's instructions bondage.
He calls sin bondage nine times in Romans 6 and never once applies that word to the Torah.

Torah brings freedom, not slavery

THE RISE OF MARCION AND THE FALL OF THE FAITHFUL

James 1:25 (NLT):
"But if you look carefully into the perfect law that sets you free, and if you do what it says and do not forget what you heard, then God will bless you for doing it."

James calls Torah "the perfect law that sets you free."

Not a burden.
Not bondage.
Freedom.

James 2:12 calls it "the law that sets you free" again.
Freedom and obedience walk together.

David repeatedly calls Torah his delight, not his prison

Psalm 119:47 (NLT):
"How I delight in Your commands. How I love them."

Psalm 119:61 (NLT):
"Even evil people try to drag me into sin, but I am firmly anchored to Your instructions."

David sees Torah as his anchor in a world of deception.
Torah protects.
Torah stabilizes.
Torah guards the heart.

Bondage does not produce delight.
Love does.

Yeshua says His commandments bring rest, not oppression

Matthew 11:28 to 30 (NLT):
"Come to Me, all of you who are weary and carry heavy burdens,

THE RISE OF MARCION AND THE FALL OF THE FAITHFUL

and I will give you rest. Take My yoke upon you. Let Me teach you... My yoke is easy to bear, and the burden I give you is light."

What burden does He give?
His teaching.
His commandments.
His Father's will.

If obedience were bondage, Yeshua could never say His yoke is easy.

Paul's rebuke in Galatians is about legalism, not Torah itself

Many use Galatians to argue that Torah is slavery.
But Paul is not attacking the Torah.
He is attacking the idea that obedience earns salvation.

Galatians 5:1 (NLT):
"So Christ has truly set us free. Now make sure that you stay free, and do not get tied up again in slavery to the law."

The slavery he describes is the belief that justification can be earned through circumcision or ritual observance.
He is refuting salvation by works, not obedience as the fruit of faith.

Paul never teaches that living righteously is bondage.
He teaches that seeking justification through works is bondage.

The solution Paul presents is not lawlessness.
The solution is Spirit empowered obedience.

Galatians 5:16 (NLT):
"Let the Holy Spirit guide your lives. Then you won't be doing what your sinful nature craves."

THE RISE OF MARCION AND THE FALL OF THE FAITHFUL

Torah cannot save.
Only Yeshua saves.
But Torah still defines righteousness.
And the Spirit empowers believers to walk in it.

The bondage of the old covenant was the bondage of a stone heart

The problem was never Torah.
The problem was the heart.

Ezekiel 36:26 to 27 (NLT):
"And I will give you a new heart... And I will put My Spirit in you so that you will follow My decrees and be careful to obey My regulations."

The Spirit produces obedience.
The new covenant restores the ability to walk in Yehovah's ways.
This is freedom, not bondage.

Yeshua taught that sin, not Torah, is the true enslaver

John 8:34 (NLT):
"Jesus replied, 'I tell you the truth, everyone who sins is a slave of sin.'"

Sin enslaves.
Torah reveals sin.
Grace breaks the chains of sin.
The Spirit leads believers into obedience.

Freedom is not the absence of commandments.
Freedom is the power to obey them with a joyful heart.

Why this matters

THE RISE OF MARCION AND THE FALL OF THE FAITHFUL

Calling Torah bondage is identical to Marcion's teaching.
Scripture never teaches it.
The apostles never taught it.
Yeshua never taught it.

Torah is freedom.
Sin is bondage.
Grace is the power to walk in the freedom of obedience.

A believer living by the Spirit is not enslaved.
They are liberated to walk in righteousness, holiness, and truth.

Torah is the path of life.
Grace brings us back onto that path.
The Spirit empowers us to walk it.

Section 4: The Torah and the Gospel Are Unified, Not Opposed

One of the greatest misunderstandings in the modern Church is the belief that the Torah and the Gospel belong to different gods, different eras, or different systems of salvation. This view came directly from Marcion. He taught that the Torah was the religion of the Jews and the Gospel was a new religion for Gentiles. Scripture never presents such a divide. The Torah and the Gospel flow from the same God, reveal the same righteousness, call for the same faith, and lead to the same covenant relationship.

The Gospel does not replace the Torah.
The Gospel fulfills the Torah.
The Gospel empowers the believer to walk in everything the Torah declared was wise, righteous, and good.

THE RISE OF MARCION AND THE FALL OF THE FAITHFUL

Paul teaches that the Gospel and the Torah proclaim the same righteousness

Romans 3:21 to 22 (NLT):
"But now God has shown us a way to be made right with Him without keeping the requirements of the law, as was promised in the writings of Moses and the prophets long ago. We are made right with God by placing our faith in Jesus Christ."

Paul does not say the Gospel replaces Torah.
He says the Gospel fulfills what Moses and the prophets promised.

The Torah pointed forward.
Grace brings the promise to life.

Romans 3:31 (NKJV):
"Do we then make void the law through faith? Certainly not. On the contrary, we establish the law."

Faith does not dismantle the Torah.
Faith confirms the Torah.

Paul teaches a single Gospel for both Jew and Gentile

Romans 1:16 (NLT):
"For I am not ashamed of this Good News about Christ. It is the power of God at work, saving everyone who believes, the Jew first and also the Gentile."

Paul does not present two different messages.
He presents one Gospel with one call and one covenant.

Ephesians 2:14 (NLT):
"For Christ Himself has brought peace to us. He united Jews and Gentiles into one people."

THE RISE OF MARCION AND THE FALL OF THE FAITHFUL

Marcion divided Jew and Gentile.
Yeshua united Jew and Gentile.

Paul's Gospel destroys any idea of a two-religion system.

The prophets foretold that the nations would follow the Torah

Isaiah 2:3 (NLT):
"People from many nations will come and say, 'Come, let us go up to the mountain of the Lord... He will teach us His ways, and we will walk in His paths.' For the Lord's teaching will go out from Zion."

The Hebrew word for teaching/instruction is Torah.
Isaiah says the nations will walk in it.

Jeremiah 31:33 (NLT):
"But this is the new covenant I will make... I will put My instructions deep within them."

The new covenant writes Torah on the heart.
Not a new law.
The same law written in a new place.

The Gospel does not abolish the commands.
It internalizes them.

Yeshua taught that the Gospel fulfills the Torah, not cancels it

Matthew 5:17 (NLT):
"I did not come to abolish the law of Moses or the writings of the prophets. No, I came to accomplish their purpose."

Yeshua does not replace Torah.
He brings Torah to its fullness.

THE RISE OF MARCION AND THE FALL OF THE FAITHFUL

He completes what it pointed toward.
He empowers what it demanded.
He embodies what it revealed.

The apostles taught that Torah and Gospel share the same foundation

Acts 24:14 (NLT):
"But I admit that I follow the Way... I worship the God of our ancestors, and firmly believe the Jewish law and everything written in the prophets."

Paul's faith in Yeshua did not replace the Torah.
It fulfilled it.

Acts 26:22 to 23 (NLT):
"I teach nothing except what the prophets and Moses said would happen."

The Gospel is not a departure from Torah.
The Gospel is the fulfillment of Torah.

Torah reveals the need for a Savior. Grace provides Him.

Romans 7:7 (NLT):
"It was the law that showed me my sin."

The Torah diagnoses sin.
The Gospel provides the cure.

The Torah reveals the righteousness of Yehovah.
The Gospel gives the Spirit so we can walk in that righteousness.

The Torah says, "This is holiness."
Grace says, "I will give you a new heart to walk in it."

The two stand together.

THE RISE OF MARCION AND THE FALL OF THE FAITHFUL

The false divide blinds believers to the fullness of the Gospel

When Torah is treated as the enemy of grace, the fullness of Scripture collapses.
Holiness becomes optional.
Obedience becomes legalism.
Covenant becomes reduced to sentiment instead of loyalty.
Discipleship is stripped of its power.

The Torah and the Gospel do not compete.
They complete each other.

The Torah reveals the nature of Yehovah.
The Gospel restores us to that nature.

The Torah defines righteousness.
The Gospel empowers righteous living.

The Torah exposes sin.
Grace forgives and conquers sin.

The Torah shows the path of life.
The Gospel places us on that path.

Why this matters

Marcion divided the Scriptures into two separate religions.
Many unknowingly repeat his mistake today.

The Bible presents one God, one revelation, one plan, one covenant, and one redeemed people walking in the unity of Torah and the Gospel.
The Gospel does not nullify the Torah.
The Gospel fulfills the Torah.

THE RISE OF MARCION AND THE FALL OF THE FAITHFUL

The Gospel empowers believers to live out the righteousness the Torah describes.

To separate them is to lose both.
To unite them is to experience the fullness of Yeshua's salvation.

Section 5: Obedience Is Not Legalism. Obedience Is the Fruit of Grace.

A common accusation against Torah observance is the claim that obeying Yehovah's commandments produces pride or legalism. The assumption is that anyone who keeps Torah believes they can earn righteousness or outperform others. Scripture teaches the opposite. True obedience flows from humility. It is the response of a heart transformed by grace. Legalism does not come from keeping Torah. Legalism comes from trying to replace grace with performance. Sin, not obedience, is what produces pride.

Scripture defines legalism as seeking justification through works

Paul never condemns obedience.
He condemns those who try to earn salvation by their own effort.

Galatians 2:16 (NLT):
"Yet we know that a person is made right with God by faith in Jesus Christ, not by obeying the law."

Paul is not attacking the Torah itself.
He is attacking the misuse of Torah.

Legalism happens when someone tries to use obedience to earn salvation.
Obedience becomes corruption when it replaces faith.
Obedience becomes beautiful when it flows from faith.

THE RISE OF MARCION AND THE FALL OF THE FAITHFUL

Yeshua condemns hypocrisy, not obedience

Matthew 23:23 (NLT):
"What sorrow awaits you teachers of religious law and you Pharisees. For you are careful to tithe even the tiniest income from your herb gardens, but you ignore the more important aspects of the law justice, mercy, and faith."

Yeshua does not rebuke them for tithing.
He rebukes them for ignoring justice, mercy, and faith.
He corrects them by saying:

"You should tithe, yes, but do not neglect the more important things."

His issue is not obedience.
His issue is pride.

Grace destroys pride by removing all grounds for boasting

Ephesians 2:8 to 9 (NLT):
"God saved you by His grace when you believed. And you cannot take credit for this."

Grace removes pride.
Grace leaves no room for boasting.
Grace humbles a believer at the foot of the cross.

A humble heart obeys.
A prideful heart rebels.

Pride does not come from Torah.
Pride comes from sin.

Obedience is the result of a new heart, not the cause of salvation

THE RISE OF MARCION AND THE FALL OF THE FAITHFUL

Ezekiel 36:26 to 27 (NLT):
"And I will give you a new heart... And I will put My Spirit in you so that you will follow My decrees."

Obedience is produced by the Spirit.

Once the heart is made new:
it desires the commandments
it delights in the commandments
it walks in the commandments

Obedience is not the price of salvation.
Obedience is the proof of salvation.

True obedience requires humility

Psalm 25:9 (NLT):
"He leads the humble in doing right, teaching them His way."

Only the humble can walk in His way.
Only the repentant can obey.

Obedience is not a way to lift oneself above others.
Obedience is the way a bowed heart lives before its King.

Those who use grace to avoid obedience display the pride the Bible condemns

2 Peter 2:19 (NLT):
"They promise freedom, but they themselves are slaves of sin."

Claiming freedom while rejecting Yehovah's instructions is the greatest arrogance.
It declares independence from the King.
It celebrates freedom from righteousness instead of freedom from sin.

THE RISE OF MARCION AND THE FALL OF THE FAITHFUL

This is the pride the apostles warn against.

Jude 1:4 (NLT):
"Some ungodly people have wormed their way into your churches, saying that God's grace allows us to live immoral lives."

Misusing grace to avoid obedience is not humility.
It is rebellion clothed in religious language.

Torah observance is not self righteousness. It is covenant faithfulness.

The prophets, the apostles, and Yeshua Himself all call believers to obedience.
Obedience is always framed as love, loyalty, gratitude, and trust.

1 John 2:3 (NLT):
"And we can be sure that we know Him if we obey His commandments."

Obedience reveals relationship.
Obedience reveals identity.
Obedience reveals the work of the Spirit.

Self righteousness boasts in its performance.
Sanctification boasts in the work of Yeshua.

Why this matters

Calling obedience "legalism" confuses two different realities.

Legalism says, "I will save myself by my works."
Obedience says, "I belong to Yeshua and I walk in His ways."

Legalism is pride.
Obedience is humility.

THE RISE OF MARCION AND THE FALL OF THE FAITHFUL

Legalism rejects grace.
Obedience is the fruit of grace.

Legalism tries to replace the Savior.
Obedience honors the Savior.

You cannot obey proudly.
You cannot disobey humbly.

Grace and Torah are not enemies.
Grace produces the very obedience that Torah describes.

Torah reveals the path of life.
Grace places us on that path.
The Spirit empowers us to walk it with humility, love, and joy.

Answering the "Yeah buts"

Whenever the subject of obedience or Torah comes up, many people respond with a familiar move. They reach for a single verse from Paul, pull it out of its context, and say, "Yeah, but Paul said..." as if that one isolated statement overturns everything Yeshua taught, everything the prophets declared, and everything the apostles lived and practiced. This is not biblical interpretation. This is cherry picking. When a person builds their theology on isolated verses instead of the whole counsel of Scripture, they create contradictions that do not exist in the Bible. They end up defending a position that cannot hold all the truth together.

Sound doctrine must make room for all the passages we covered in this section.
If a theology cannot hold every one of these truths at the same table, that theology is flawed.

THE RISE OF MARCION AND THE FALL OF THE FAITHFUL

Truth does not contradict truth.

Cherry picking Paul always produces contradictions

People often quote Paul's statements about the law without reading the paragraph, chapter, or letter they are found in. They ignore Paul's own declarations that the Torah is holy, just, good, spiritual, and established by faith. They ignore his teaching that grace trains us to obey. They ignore his warnings against lawlessness. They ignore his love for the commandments. They ignore the fact that he lived Torah faithfully, kept the feasts, upheld the Temple, and defended himself by saying he taught nothing contrary to Moses.

A theology built on isolated verses from Paul will always collapse under the weight of the rest of Scripture.

Context reveals Paul never opposed Torah obedience

When Paul condemns "works," he condemns the attempt to earn justification.
He never condemns Spirit empowered obedience as the fruit of salvation.

When Paul opposes "the law," he opposes the misuse of Torah as a ladder to climb toward righteousness.
He never calls righteous living bondage.
He never treats holiness as a burden.
He never describes obedience as a threat to grace.

When Paul speaks of "freedom," he speaks of freedom from sin, not freedom from righteousness.

When Paul uses the word "law" in a negative sense, he almost always refers to:

- the law used as a means of justification

THE RISE OF MARCION AND THE FALL OF THE FAITHFUL

- the law misapplied through human traditions
- the law in the hands of the sinful nature
- the law as a tutor pointing to Messiah
- the condemnation produced by breaking the law

He never attacks the law itself.
He attacks the misuse of it.

A doctrine that cannot honor all of Scripture is already broken. Truth does not need to ignore verses or explain them away. It holds everything the Word says in one united picture. Yeshua said He did not come to abolish the Torah, and He taught that obedience is wisdom, not bondage. He told us plainly that His teaching comes from the Father, and He defined love for God as keeping His commandments. Paul never undermined that. He said faith establishes the Torah, that grace trains us to reject sin and live righteously, and that the Spirit fulfills the Torah's righteous requirement in us. He described the Torah as holy, just, good, spiritual, and a gift of freedom. According to Scripture, sin is bondage, not Torah.

The prophets said the new covenant would write God's instructions on the heart, not remove them. Obedience is the fruit of salvation, not the cause of it. Lawlessness marks deception, not maturity. And the prophets declare that in the Messianic age, the nations will come to Jerusalem to learn the Torah. All of this matters because Yeshua is the Word made flesh. He did not erase the Word. He revealed it. Any theology that cannot hold all of these truths at once is too small. The Scriptures do not need to bend to fit man's doctrine. Our doctrine must bow to the Scriptures.

If someone's "yeah but Paul said" theology cannot hold all these truths without contradiction, the theology must change. Scripture does not bend around our traditions. Our traditions must bend around Scripture.

Cherry picked theories collapse when held up to the whole Bible

People often build arguments like these:

"Yeah, but Paul said we are not under law."
Context shows he means we are not under its condemnation.

"Yeah, but Paul said the law was a burden."
Paul never said this. Ever.

"Yeah, but Paul said the law brings death."
He says sin brings death. The law exposes sin.

"Yeah, but Paul said circumcision means nothing."
He was correcting those who pursued it for justification, not obedience.

"Yeah, but Paul said Christ is the end of the law."
The Greek word telos means goal, purpose, completion, not termination.

Every "yeah but" collapses when read in context.

The apostles never needed to correct Torah obedience. They corrected lawlessness and legalism.

The apostles never rebuked someone for keeping the commandments.
They rebuked people who tried to earn salvation.
They rebuked people who added human traditions.
They rebuked people who twisted grace into sin.
They rebuked people who taught lawlessness.

THE RISE OF MARCION AND THE FALL OF THE FAITHFUL

Their correction is always aimed at the ditch on either side of the road, never at the road itself.

Truth is not threatened by obedience. Truth is threatened by distortion.

The "yeah buts" arise because believers have been trained to defend a theology that cannot hold the whole Bible together. They scramble for isolated verses because their system collapses when confronted with the fullness of Scripture.

A theology that requires ignoring the words of Yeshua, dismissing the prophets, minimizing the Torah, and misusing Paul is not biblical theology.

A sound theology is wide enough to embrace all that Scripture says.
It does not twist Paul to silence Moses.
It does not pit grace against Torah.
It does not use isolated verses to overturn the words of Yeshua.
It does not reduce obedience to legalism.

Truth is unified.
Grace and Torah stand together.
Faith and obedience walk together.
Yeshua and the Father speak with the same voice.

If the "yeah buts" cannot sit at the table with all these truths, they do not belong at the table of sound doctrine.

THE RISE OF MARCION AND THE FALL OF THE FAITHFUL

Chapter 24 Denial of Yeshua's True Identity

Marcion's final and most dangerous error was his attack on the identity of Yeshua. Once he rejected the Torah and embraced Gnostic dualism, he could no longer accept the truth that Yeshua is Yehovah. Instead, he created a new Jesus, separated from Israel, disconnected from the prophets, and detached from the God of Abraham, Isaac, and Jacob. This false Jesus still appears in many pulpits today. Whenever believers separate Yeshua from His Jewish identity, His Torah, His Father's covenant, or His own teaching, they unknowingly echo Marcion's error.

The true Gospel reveals one consistent message.
Yeshua is Yehovah in the flesh.
The Word came forth from the Father.
The Spirit is the breath of Yehovah.
There is no division in the nature of God.

Yeshua reveals the same God who spoke at Sinai

Exodus 3:14 (NLT):
"God replied to Moses, 'I AM WHO I AM. Say this to the people of Israel: I AM has sent me to you.'"

John 8:58 (NLT):
"Jesus answered, 'I tell you the truth, before Abraham was even born, I AM.'"

Yeshua does not claim similarity.
He claims identity.

He does not say He represents the God of Israel.
He says He is the I AM who spoke to Moses.

THE RISE OF MARCION AND THE FALL OF THE FAITHFUL

Marcion rejected this.
Many modern teachers soften it.
But the text is clear.

Yeshua's authority is the authority of Yehovah

John 5:19 (NLT):
"The Son can do nothing by Himself. He does only what He sees the Father doing."

This is not separation.
This is unity of action, unity of nature, and unity of purpose.

John 10:30 (NLT):
"The Father and I are one."

Yeshua does not speak as a second god or a new deity.
He speaks as the visible revelation of the invisible God.

Yeshua receives worship that belongs only to Yehovah

Matthew 14:33 (NLT):
"Then the disciples worshiped Him. 'You really are the Son of God,' they exclaimed."

Revelation 5:12 to 14 (NLT):
The Lamb receives worship alongside the One on the throne.

Scripture forbids worship of anyone except Yehovah.
Yet Yeshua receives worship without rebuke.

The only possible explanation is the one the apostles give.
Yeshua shares the identity of Yehovah.

THE RISE OF MARCION AND THE FALL OF THE FAITHFUL

Yeshua forgives sin as Yehovah alone can forgive

Mark 2:5 to 7 (NLT):
"'My child, your sins are forgiven.'
'This is blasphemy. Only God can forgive sins.'"

The religious leaders understood the claim.
Forgiving sin is divine authority.
Yeshua does not deny it.
He demonstrates it.

Yeshua exercises the divine prerogatives of Yehovah

Only Yehovah:
- stills storms
- walks on the waters of chaos
- commands angels
- judges the nations
- raises the dead
- gives life
- writes the covenant
- sends the Spirit

Yet Yeshua performs each one.
Not as a secondary deity.
Not as a created being.
But as Yehovah revealed.

Marcion's "Jesus" denied the Tanakh. The biblical Yeshua fulfills it.

Luke 24:44 (NLT):
"Everything written about Me in the Law of Moses and the Prophets and in the Psalms must be fulfilled."

The biblical Yeshua stands on:
the Torah

THE RISE OF MARCION AND THE FALL OF THE FAITHFUL

the Prophets
the Writings
the promises made to Israel

The Marcionite Jesus stood on nothing.

Modern Christianity often repeats this mistake when it:
- detaches Jesus from Israel
- treats the Old Testament as irrelevant
- rejects the Torah
- ignores the prophetic timeline

The real Yeshua is inseparable from the Scriptures He wrote through Moses and the prophets.

Denying Yeshua's divinity always leads to denying His authority

Every false version of Jesus throughout history has shared a common feature.
He becomes less than Yehovah.
He becomes a teacher.
He becomes a prophet.
He becomes a guide.
He becomes a moral example.

But He is no longer the eternal Word made flesh.

When this happens, His commandments lose weight.
His Torah loses relevance.
His authority becomes negotiable.
His identity becomes symbolic.

THE RISE OF MARCION AND THE FALL OF THE FAITHFUL

His Gospel becomes sentimental.
His return becomes optional.

A diminished Jesus produces a diminished faith.

The apostles built the Gospel on the identity of Yeshua as Yehovah

2 Corinthians 4:6 (NLT):
"For God, who said, 'Let there be light in the darkness,' has made this light shine in our hearts through the face of Jesus Christ."

The God of creation is revealed in the face of Yeshua.
This is the apostolic Gospel.

Colossians 1:15 to 17 (NLT):
"Christ is the visible image of the invisible God.
He existed before anything was created and is supreme over all creation."

This destroys every form of Marcionism.
It destroys every form of Gnosticism.
It destroys every attempt to reduce Yeshua to less than Yehovah.

Why this matters

Once the identity of Yeshua is distorted, everything else collapses:

- Torah loses relevance
- grace loses definition
- obedience loses purpose
- holiness loses meaning
- covenant loses continuity
- the Gospel loses power

The biblical faith stands on this unshakeable truth.
The same Yehovah who thundered at Sinai came in the person of

THE RISE OF MARCION AND THE FALL OF THE FAITHFUL

Yeshua to redeem His people.
He did not abolish His own Word.
He fulfilled it.
He wrote it.
He empowered His followers to walk in it.

Rejecting Yeshua's true identity always leads to rejecting His commands.
Confessing Yeshua as Yehovah restores the unity of Scripture, the beauty of the Gospel, and the authority of the King who calls His people into covenant love.

For a deep dive into this subject, please consider my book: *Mark My Words: Yeshua is Yehovah*. It is a chapter-by-chapter examination of Mark, in his own words, of who Yeshua is.

THE RISE OF MARCION AND THE FALL OF THE FAITHFUL

Chapter 25 Gnosticism and Dualism

Marcion's rejection of the Torah did not occur in a vacuum. His ideas took root in a world already shaped by Gnosticism. Gnosticism taught that matter is evil, the physical world is corrupt, and the true God is distant from creation. Only hidden knowledge could save a person from the material realm. This worldview stood in direct opposition to Scripture, which teaches that creation is good, the Torah is holy, the body matters, and Yehovah works within His creation to redeem it.

When Marcion rejected the Torah and the God of the Hebrew Scriptures, he embraced a dualistic worldview. He taught that the "God of the Old Testament" was a lesser deity who created the physical world and imposed laws on humanity, while the "God of Jesus" was a higher spiritual being who came to free people from the material order. This dualism was a direct inheritance from Gnosticism. Because Marcion gained influence, his teachings spread into Christian thinking and still influence it today.

Gnosticism despised the physical world. Torah celebrates it.

Genesis 1:31 (NLT):
"Then God looked over all He had made, and He saw that it was very good."

Gnostics taught that the material world is a prison of the soul.
The Torah teaches that creation is good.
Gnostics tried to escape creation.
Torah teaches believers to steward creation.

THE RISE OF MARCION AND THE FALL OF THE FAITHFUL

The God of Israel is not distant.
He walks with Adam.
He appears to Abraham.
He speaks with Moses.
He dwells among His people.

Gnostic gods do not do this.
Only the true God does.

Gnosticism rejected the body. The Gospel affirms resurrection.

1 Corinthians 6:19 (NLT):
"Your body is the temple of the Holy Spirit."

Gnosticism taught that salvation came from escaping the body.
The Gospel teaches resurrection of the body.

Romans 8:11 (NLT):
"The Spirit of God... will give life to your mortal bodies."

The physical body is honored by Yehovah.
He formed it, redeemed it, indwells it, and will resurrect it.

Dualism denies this truth.

Gnosticism rejected obedience. Scripture says obedience is the fruit of truth.

2 John 1:6 (NLT):
"Love means doing what God has commanded us."

Gnostics taught that salvation came through hidden knowledge, not obedience.
Marcion absorbed this idea.
He taught that commandments belonged to a lesser god.

THE RISE OF MARCION AND THE FALL OF THE FAITHFUL

But Scripture says:
knowledge without obedience is deception
faith without obedience is dead
love without obedience is false

The apostles fought this error fiercely.

1 John 2:4 (NLT):
"If someone claims, 'I know God,' but does not obey His commandments, that person is a liar."

Gnostic antinomianism leads to lawlessness.
The apostles expose it as counterfeit faith.

Gnosticism divided God into two beings. Scripture declares the unity of Yehovah.

Deuteronomy 6:4 (NLT):
"Listen, O Israel. The Lord is our God, the Lord alone."

Gnostics divided God into two beings:
a lesser creator and a superior spiritual deity.

Marcion repeated this.
He said the God of the Torah was not the Father of Yeshua.

The apostles reject this entirely.

John 10:30 (NLT):
"The Father and I are one."

There are not two gods.
There is one.
The same God who gave the Torah sent His Son to fulfill it.

Gnosticism denied that the Messiah came in the flesh.

THE RISE OF MARCION AND THE FALL OF THE FAITHFUL

1 John 4:2 to 3 (NLT):
"If a person claiming to be a prophet does not acknowledge the truth about Jesus, that person is not from God."

The Gnostics believed the physical world was corrupt and the human body was a prison for the soul. Because of that, many of them denied that Yeshua came in a real human body. They could not accept a Messiah who walked, bled, suffered, died, and rose again in flesh. Yet this is exactly what the Gospel affirms. The incarnation is not symbolic. It is real flesh, real blood, real suffering, real death, and real resurrection. To deny the humanity of Yeshua is to deny the Gospel itself. That error came from Gnosticism, and it spread quickly through the circles influenced by Marcion.

Marcion's rejection of the Torah opened the door to the same kind of dualistic thinking. Once he separated the New Testament from the Old, it was easy for him to divide everything into two competing categories. Torah became bad and grace became good. The physical world became corrupt and the spiritual became pure. Obedience became bondage and knowledge became freedom. This split did not come from Scripture. It came from Gnostic philosophy.

The tragedy is that many modern Christians unknowingly echo these same ideas. Whenever someone dismisses the Old Testament or treats the incarnation like a secondary doctrine, they repeat Gnostic thinking. When believers distrust the physical world as if God did not call creation good, or when they speak of the commandments as if obedience were something oppressive, they are following a different teacher. When grace is described as a release from holiness instead of the power to walk in it, the shadow of Gnosticism is still present.

THE RISE OF MARCION AND THE FALL OF THE FAITHFUL

None of these ideas are biblical. They are leftovers from the ancient world, dressed in Christian vocabulary. Scripture teaches something far different. It calls creation good, the Torah holy, the Incarnation essential, and obedience the joyful response of those who love God. When we return to the Word, the fog of Gnostic dualism begins to lift.

The apostles fought Gnosticism because it distorts the Gospel

Colossians 2:8 (NLT):
"Don't let anyone capture you with empty philosophies and high sounding nonsense that come from human thinking and from the spiritual powers of this world, rather than from Christ."

Paul wrote to combat early forms of Gnosticism:
secret knowledge
worship of angels
dualistic thinking
legalism divorced from faith
lawlessness disguised as spirituality

The apostles never separated Yeshua from the Torah.
They never separated faith from obedience.
They never separated the physical from the spiritual.
They never separated the Father from the Son.

Why this matters

Gnosticism and Marcionism form the backbone of many modern theological errors.
Whenever Scripture is divided, whenever Torah is rejected, whenever obedience is dismissed, whenever the physical world is

despised, whenever knowledge replaces repentance, the fingerprints of Gnosticism are visible.

Yehovah's truth is unified.
His Word is unified.
His covenant is unified.
His character is unified.
His Son is the perfect revelation of the same God who gave the Torah at Sinai.

To embrace the Gospel is to reject dualism.
To follow Yeshua is to follow the God of Israel.
To walk in the Spirit is to walk in the same righteousness the Torah reveals.

Chapter 26 Subversion of Canon

Marcion's attack on the Bible was not limited to theology. He attempted to rewrite the Scriptures themselves. His strategy was simple but devastating. If he could reshape the canon, he could reshape the Gospel. If he could remove the Hebrew Scriptures and mutilate the apostolic writings, he could promote a version of Christianity disconnected from the God of Israel.

This was not a minor disagreement.
This was a direct assault on the foundation of the faith.

Marcion's Canon: The First Attempt to Rewrite Scripture

Marcion created the earliest known "Christian canon," but it was a canon built through subtraction, not preservation. His canon consisted of:

- a mutilated version of Luke
- ten edited Pauline epistles
- total rejection of the Hebrew Scriptures
- complete separation from Israel's story, covenant, and God

He removed everything that connected Yeshua to the Old Testament. He removed every Old Testament quotation. He removed genealogies, prophecies, and the birth narrative. He deleted references to Abraham, David, Moses, and the prophets. His goal was clear.

Remove Israel.
Remove covenant.

THE RISE OF MARCION AND THE FALL OF THE FAITHFUL

Remove Torah.
Remove the God of the Tanakh.

And once those foundations were gone, he could insert his own theology.

The Early Church Rejected Marcion Completely

Every early Christian writer condemned Marcion's canon.

Tertullian (AD 200)

Tertullian devotes several books to refuting Marcion's edits.

Tertullian, *Against Marcion* 4.2:
"He mutilated the Gospel that he used, removing whatever he did not like."

Tertullian exposes how Marcion:

- cut out the birth of Yeshua
- cut out fulfilled prophecy
- cut out the Law and Prophets
- cut out anything affirming Yeshua as the Messiah of Israel

Irenaeus (AD 175)

Irenaeus attacked Marcion's rejection of the Old Testament, calling it a rejection of the God who inspired Scripture.

Irenaeus, *Against Heresies* 3.12.12:
"Marcion... mutilated the scriptures to support his own doctrine."

Epiphanius (AD 350)

Epiphanius preserved long lists of verses Marcion deleted.

THE RISE OF MARCION AND THE FALL OF THE FAITHFUL

Epiphanius, *Panarion* 42.11:
"He removed what he wished, and added what served his purpose."

The early Church did not tolerate a selective canon.
They guarded the Scriptures because the Scriptures guard the Gospel.

The Hebrew Scriptures Were the Bible of Yeshua and the Apostles

Marcion claimed the Old Testament was irrelevant.
The apostles taught the opposite.

The Hebrew Scriptures were the Bible of Yeshua. When He taught, He quoted Moses, David, and the prophets. When He confronted temptation, He answered with "It is written." They were also the Bible of Paul. Every doctrine he preached, including grace, faith, redemption, and resurrection, came straight from the Torah and the Prophets. Peter stood on the same foundation, calling Israel to repentance by appealing to Joel, Isaiah, and the Psalms. And the early Church relied on those same Scriptures. When you read the sermons in Acts, every message is built on the Hebrew Bible. There was no New Testament yet. The entire movement of The Way was launched from the Scriptures that many believers now treat as optional.

The phrase "the Scriptures" in the New Testament always refers to the Tanakh.

Paul wrote:
"All Scripture is inspired by God" (2 Timothy 3:16, NLT).
The only Scripture he had in hand was the Old Testament.

When you remove the Hebrew Scriptures, you remove the foundation of the Gospel. The apostles never treated the Old Testament as optional; it was the very soil the New Testament grew

THE RISE OF MARCION AND THE FALL OF THE FAITHFUL

out of. Every major truth we cherish today is rooted there. You cannot understand Messiah, covenant, sacrifice, priesthood, redemption, kingdom, righteousness, sin, salvation, judgment, resurrection, or atonement without the Scriptures that define those words. Tear away the Torah and the Prophets, and the entire message of Yeshua collapses. The New Testament does not replace the Old ... it depends on it. It stands or falls with it.

This is why Marcion targeted the canon. He knew that if he could sever the church from the Hebrew Bible, he could reshape the Gospel into his own image. And nowhere is his strategy clearer than in the version of Luke's Gospel he produced. Marcion's edits speak louder than his sermons. He stripped away the genealogy because it tied Yeshua to Israel. He deleted every fulfillment passage because it showed continuity with the prophets. He removed prophecies, references to Abraham, connections to David, mentions of the Law, and anything that rooted Yeshua in Jewish identity. He even removed the infancy narratives because they established the Messiah promised long ago.

Piece by piece, he cut out the Old Testament God, the covenant story, and the prophetic framework that makes sense of the Gospel. When he was finished, the Jesus who remained was not the Messiah of Israel but a detached spiritual figure with no roots, no history, and no covenant. And that was the point. Marcion needed a different canon because he believed in a different Christ. Once the Scriptures were rewritten, his theology slid neatly into place.

The tragedy is that many modern Christians have unknowingly inherited a similar pattern. Whenever the Old Testament is sidelined, ignored, or declared irrelevant, Marcion's shadow returns. If the church loses the Scriptures Yeshua loved, it loses the very Gospel He came to fulfill.

THE RISE OF MARCION AND THE FALL OF THE FAITHFUL

Why Canon Matters

Canon is not something the Church invented. Canon is something the Church recognized. The early believers did not sit down and decide which writings had authority. They simply acknowledged the ones that already carried the voice of the apostles. Marcion tried to flip that pattern. Instead of letting Scripture shape his theology, he tried to shape Scripture around his theology. That is always the dividing line. Either your theology submits to the Word, or the Word gets trimmed to fit your theology. Marcion chose the second path. The apostles taught the first.

There is a popular idea today that Marcion forced the early Church to define the canon. The historical evidence shows something very different. Long before Marcion appeared, the four Gospels were already circulating as a unified collection. Paul's letters were already gathered and read together. Apostolic writings were being used in worship, and bishops across different regions were teaching from the same books. When heresies appeared, they were judged by these writings. And everywhere you look, the Hebrew Scriptures were treated as fully authoritative.

Marcion did not spark the creation of the canon. He forced the Church to defend the canon it already knew and cherished. His attack did not produce something new. It simply revealed what the early believers had been standing on since the beginning.

Modern Echoes of Marcion's Canon

Marcion's spirit still lives when people say:

THE RISE OF MARCION AND THE FALL OF THE FAITHFUL

- "The Old Testament no longer applies."
- "We only follow the words of Jesus."
- "Paul rejected the Law."
- "Israel is irrelevant."
- "We are a New Testament church."
- "The Law was nailed to the cross."
- "The God of the Old Testament is harsh."
- "The Old Testament is for Jews only."

Every one of these ideas traces back to Marcion's attempt to create a new canon.

Modern Christianity repeats Marcion when it lifts the New Testament out of its Old Testament foundation.

The early Church won this issue because they refused to let Marcion drive a wedge between the Scriptures and the Savior. They would not separate Yeshua from the Law and the Prophets because those writings pointed to Him. They would not pull the New Testament away from the Old because the two speak with one voice. They would not rip the apostles away from their Jewish identity because their calling and authority came through Israel's covenant. They would not preach a Gospel detached from Israel because the Gospel is the fulfillment of God's promises to Israel. And they refused to read Scripture outside of its original context because they knew that truth is lost when the roots are cut.

The early believers fought for the whole canon because only the whole canon reveals the whole Messiah.

Conclusion

Subverting the canon is not an academic disagreement.
It is a spiritual attack on the authority of Scripture, the identity of the Messiah, and the foundation of the Gospel. When the canon is divided, distorted, or diminished, everything collapses:

- Theology
- Identity
- Covenant
- Discipleship
- Truth

Marcion tried to create a Bible without Israel.
The early Church rejected him.
We must do the same.

Chapter 27 Severing the Apostles from Their Jewish Context

One of the most destructive errors introduced by Marcion and repeated today is the attempt to detach the apostles from their Jewish identity, Jewish practice, and Jewish worldview. When this happens, the Gospel becomes distorted. The apostles become strangers to their own Scriptures. The Messiah becomes disconnected from the promises of God. And the faith becomes unrecognizable to its original audience.

Marcion taught that the apostles abandoned Torah and Jewish life when they followed Yeshua. Modern theology often repeats this without realizing its origin. But the New Testament shows the opposite. The apostles remained deeply rooted in the Hebrew Scriptures, Jewish tradition, Temple life, synagogue worship, and the rhythm of Israel's festivals.

The apostles did not convert away from Judaism.
They embraced the fulfillment of their faith in the Jewish Messiah.

The Apostles Lived as Torah-Faithful Jews

They continued going to the Temple at the appointed hours

Acts 3:1 (NLT):
"Peter and John went to the Temple one afternoon to take part in the three o'clock prayer service."
Approximate date: AD 30–35

They did not abandon prayer times. They kept them.

THE RISE OF MARCION AND THE FALL OF THE FAITHFUL

They continued keeping the festivals

Acts 20:16 (NLT):
"Paul was eager to get to Jerusalem, if possible, in time for the Festival of Pentecost."
Approximate date: AD 55

Paul hurried to celebrate Shavuot because he was still a Torah-keeping Jew.

Jewish believers in Jerusalem remained Torah-faithful

Acts 21:20 (NLT):
"You see, brother, how many thousands of Jews have also believed, and they all follow the law of Moses very seriously."
Approximate date: AD 57

Thousands of Jewish followers of Yeshua continued keeping Torah faithfully.

Paul himself lived in obedience to Torah

Acts 24:14 (NLT):
"But I admit that I follow the Way… I worship the God of our ancestors, and I firmly believe the Jewish law and everything written in the prophets."
Approximate date: AD 57

He did not reject the Law and Prophets.
He affirmed them.

Acts 25:8 (NLT):
"Paul insisted, 'I have done nothing wrong against the Jewish law…'"
Approximate date: AD 58

THE RISE OF MARCION AND THE FALL OF THE FAITHFUL

Paul declares his innocence under Torah because he lived by it.

Paul kept the Nazarite vow

Acts 18:18 (NLT):
"...Paul stayed in Corinth... Then he shaved his head according to Jewish custom, marking the end of a vow."
Approximate date: AD 50–52

This is straight from Numbers 6.
Paul didn't call it bondage.
He practiced it.

Paul offered sacrifices at the Temple

Acts 21:23–26 (NLT) shows Paul not only participating but sponsoring sacrifices for others.
Approximate date: AD 57

This is impossible if Paul believed Torah was abolished.

The New Testament Writers Thought Like Jews

The apostles:

- quoted the Tanakh constantly
- used Jewish idioms
- understood Temple imagery
- interpreted Yeshua's life through Torah and the Prophets
- preached from the Hebrew Scriptures
- taught in synagogues
- lived among Jewish communities

They never thought of themselves as starting a new religion.
They believed they were living in the renewal of Israel promised by the prophets.

THE RISE OF MARCION AND THE FALL OF THE FAITHFUL

Removing the Apostles From Their Jewish Identity Creates a False Gospel

When you strip the apostles from their Jewish identity, you create a Gospel they would never recognize. The moment their roots are cut, the whole story begins to shift. The Gospel loses its connection to prophecy, as if the promises of Isaiah, Jeremiah, and Moses have nothing to do with Yeshua. The teachings of Yeshua become abstract sayings instead of covenant instructions spoken by Israel's Messiah. Grace becomes detached from covenant, floating in the air with no anchor in God's long-term plan. Faith becomes separated from obedience, as if trusting God and following Him were two different things. The Scriptures begin to look divided rather than united, and Christianity starts to appear like a Gentile invention instead of the fulfillment of everything Yehovah promised to Israel.

This is not a small error. It is the exact distortion Marcion intended. He wanted a Gospel with no Israel, a Messiah with no covenant, and a faith with no roots. Once the apostles are removed from their Jewish identity, his vision slips quietly into place.

The true Gospel is not a break from Biblical-Judaism.
It is the flowering of it.

Yeshua is the Messiah promised to Israel.
The apostles preached from Israel's Scriptures.
The early Church lived as a continuation of Israel's faith.
And the nations were grafted in, not inserted above Israel.

Scholarly and Historical Support

Papias (AD 95–120)
Describes Matthew writing in Hebrew for Jewish believers, proving early Jewish context.

THE RISE OF MARCION AND THE FALL OF THE FAITHFUL

Justin Martyr (AD 150–165)
Calls believers "the true Israel," affirming continuity, not replacement.

Irenaeus (AD 175–190)
Connects the Gospel to the promises given to the patriarchs.

Epiphanius (AD 350)
Records that Jewish followers of Yeshua continued Torah observance for centuries.

Jerome (AD 380)
Notes Hebrew versions of Matthew used among Jewish believers in his day.

Not one early Christian source describes the apostles as abandoning Torah.
That narrative begins with Marcion.

Why This Matters Today

When modern Christians remove the apostles from their Jewish context, they inherit a Marcionite lens without realizing it. They begin to assume:

- Torah is irrelevant
- the Old Testament is less important
- Jewish identity is optional
- the Gospel is detached from Israel
- Yeshua overturned Moses

But the apostles preached the opposite.

They proclaimed a Jewish Messiah.
They upheld the Torah as God's instruction.

THE RISE OF MARCION AND THE FALL OF THE FAITHFUL

They taught the nations to worship the God of Israel.
They viewed the Gospel as the fulfillment of the Hebrew Scriptures.

To sever the apostles from their Jewish identity is to sever the Gospel from its foundation.

Chapter 28 Spiritual Elitism and Secret Knowledge

One of the most destructive errors that emerged in the early centuries and still circulates today is the idea that true spirituality belongs only to a select group of insiders who possess higher revelation, deeper insight, or secret knowledge unavailable to ordinary believers. This mindset is the heartbeat of Gnosticism, and it is the same spirit that shaped Marcion's teachings.

Marcion claimed he alone understood the true Gospel.
He claimed the apostles misunderstood Yeshua.
He claimed the Church fell into error almost immediately.
He claimed the Hebrew Scriptures were inferior.
He claimed to possess revelation higher than Scripture itself.

This is spiritual elitism at its core.
Truth for the few.
Confusion for the many.

Gnosticism promised knowledge that saves.
The Gospel gives faith that saves.

Gnostic Elitism and Biblical Revelation Compared

Gnosticism taught that:

- salvation came through secret knowledge
- only the enlightened could understand truth
- Scripture contained hidden layers only initiates could unlock
- ordinary believers were spiritually inferior
- the physical world was corrupt, so knowledge mattered more than obedience

THE RISE OF MARCION AND THE FALL OF THE FAITHFUL

- authority rested in a special teacher, not in Scripture

This worldview shaped Marcion's approach to the faith.

Biblical revelation teaches the opposite.

Proverbs 8:9 (NLT):
"My words are plain to anyone with understanding, clear to those with knowledge."

Psalm 119:130 (NLT):
"The teaching of your word gives light, so even the simple can understand."

Yeshua never hid truth behind secret doors.

John 18:20 (NLT):
"I have spoken openly to the world. I said nothing in secret."

The Gospel is not an elite code.
It is a revelation for every believer.

The Apostles Condemned Secret Knowledge

Paul warned repeatedly against elitist spiritual claims.

Paul rejects hidden wisdom claims

Colossians 2:18 to 19 (NLT):
"Do not let anyone who delights in pretending to be humble and worshiping angels say you are wrong. Their sinful minds have made them proud, and they are not connected to Christ."

Gnostics claimed visions, angels, and esoteric insight.
Paul called it pride.

Paul rejects speculative teachings

THE RISE OF MARCION AND THE FALL OF THE FAITHFUL

1 Timothy 1:4 (NLT):
"Do not let them waste their time in endless discussion of myths and spiritual pedigrees. These things only lead to meaningless speculation."

Gnosticism fed on hidden truths.
Paul exposed them as empty imagination.

Paul rejects competing revelations

Galatians 1:8 (NLT):
"Let God's curse fall on anyone who preaches a different kind of Good News than the one we preached to you."

There is no elite version of the Gospel.
There is no higher revelation.

John condemns secret knowledge cults

1 John 2:20 to 21 (NLT):
"You are not like that, for the Holy One has given you his Spirit, and all of you know the truth."

Gnostics claimed special anointing.
John said the Spirit teaches all believers.

Peter condemns teachers who brag about special insight

2 Peter 2:18 (NLT):
"They brag about themselves with empty, foolish boasting."

Gnostics offered elite knowledge.
Peter called it foolishness.

THE RISE OF MARCION AND THE FALL OF THE FAITHFUL

Marcion and Gnosticism Shared the Same Error

Marcion believed he alone truly understood Yeshua. That was the heart of his error. He convinced himself that he had insight no one else possessed, that he alone knew the real God, and that he alone understood Paul. In his mind, the apostles had misunderstood the Gospel, the early Church had been deceived, and the Scriptures themselves needed his corrections. Once a man reaches that level of spiritual pride, every safeguard collapses. Marcion stopped listening to the Word and started editing the Word, which is always the beginning of deception.

This was spiritual elitism.
It still appears today. If you have two or more of these flags, be wary. If someone says:

- "Only I have the real revelation."
- "The Church got it wrong."
- "The Bible is corrupt."
- "The apostles misunderstood Jesus."
- "True believers follow my teaching."

These ideas are not new.
They echo Marcion and Gnosticism.

The Biblical Model: Revelation for All Believers

The Bible gives a clear picture.

1. God reveals truth openly

Deuteronomy 29:29 (NLT):
"The revealed things belong to us and our children forever."

THE RISE OF MARCION AND THE FALL OF THE FAITHFUL

God reveals truth for His people.
Not for an elite inner circle.

2. Scripture is clear and accessible

Psalm 19:7 (NLT):
"The instructions of the Lord are perfect, reviving the soul. The decrees of the Lord are trustworthy, making wise the simple."

The Torah was given to ordinary families and communities.

3. The Spirit teaches every believer

John 14:26 (NLT):
"The Father will send the Advocate. He will teach you everything."

Not some believers.
All believers.

4. Scripture protects against elitist deception

2 Timothy 3:16 to 17 (NLT):
"All Scripture is inspired by God. God uses it to prepare and equip his people."

Scripture equips everyone who follows Yeshua.

Modern Forms of Spiritual Elitism

The same spirit shows up today whenever someone claims they have revelation that goes beyond Scripture or hidden meanings that only their group can decode. You hear it when teachers speak as if their prophetic authority can override the written Word or when they imply that spiritual depth comes from secret knowledge instead of obedient faith. It appears when people talk about deeper truths unavailable to ordinary believers or when salvation is treated as something gained through insight rather than through Yeshua.

THE RISE OF MARCION AND THE FALL OF THE FAITHFUL

Whenever a teacher says, "Only I can show you the real meaning," you are hearing the old voice of Gnosticism. It is the same spirit that deceived Marcion, only dressed in modern language.

Why This Matters for Canon, Torah, and the Gospel

Spiritual elitism was at the heart of Marcion's error. He believed he stood above the apostles and possessed insight no one else could see. That pride led him down a path that always produces destruction. His elitism pushed him to:

- reject the Hebrew Scriptures
- mutilate the Gospel of Luke
- edit Paul's letters to fit his theology
- deny the Jewish identity of Yeshua
- invent a false system with two gods
- oppose the apostles' teaching
- elevate his own revelations over the Word of God

Once a man believes he alone has the truth, he will eventually rewrite the Scriptures to match his own image.

And the same thing happens whenever spiritual elitism enters the Church. It always leads toward:

- distortion of the canon
- rejection of God's commandments
- separation from Israel and the covenant
- confusion about who Yeshua truly is

THE RISE OF MARCION AND THE FALL OF THE FAITHFUL

- counterfeit versions of the Gospel
- movements built around personalities rather than truth
- divided congregations and wounded believers
- deception that spreads quietly but deeply

This is the pattern of every elitist movement from the first century to today. It is the fruit of pride, not the fruit of the Spirit.

The Gospel does not create a class of "special ones" with insider access.
It creates a humble and faithful people who walk in the light, cling to the Word, and obey the Messiah with sincerity of heart.

Conclusion

Spiritual elitism replaces:

Scripture with secret insight
Obedience with speculation
Humility with pride
Faith with superior knowledge
Community with isolated circles

Marcion embraced this mindset and fell into deception.
Gnosticism embraced this mindset and collapsed under pride.
Modern believers fall into it whenever they elevate private revelation over the Word of God.

The Gospel of Yeshua is for the humble, the obedient, and the faithful.

THE RISE OF MARCION AND THE FALL OF THE FAITHFUL

Truth belongs to those who fear the Lord, not those who claim secret keys.

Chapter 29 Misused Scriptures Explained in Context

A great deal of confusion in the modern Church comes from a handful of verses pulled out of context and used as proof that Torah was abolished. You have heard the pattern many times. Someone quotes half a verse, skips everything around it, and builds an entire doctrine on a fragment. No background. No audience. No author's intent. No connection to the words of Yeshua. When Scripture is handled that way, almost any meaning can be forced into it.

This is not new. Marcion did the same thing in the second century. He cut Scripture apart, kept the pieces he liked, and threw away the ones that challenged his theology. He read verses in isolation, ignored everything that pointed to obedience, and used Paul to contradict Yeshua. Many of the same misinterpretations circulating today trace straight back to his approach. The names have changed. The packaging is cleaner. But the method is the same. When you isolate verses from their context, you can make them say whatever you want.

The solution has not changed either. Read the Word in its full setting. Let Scripture explain Scripture. Anchor everything in the heart of God revealed from Genesis to Revelation. When you do that, the confusion disappears. The Bible never contradicts itself. The God of the Old Testament is the God of the New. The faith of Abraham is the faith of the apostles. The same Spirit who spoke through Moses empowered the apostles to walk in obedience after the resurrection. And the New Covenant never removed God's commandments. It placed them inside the heart, just as Jeremiah promised and Hebrews confirms.

Before we walk through the most misused passages, there are a few truths Scripture repeats everywhere. Yeshua kept the commandments and taught His disciples to do the same. Paul never disagreed with Yeshua. The apostles continued living Torah obedient lives long after the resurrection. Scripture never calls Torah a burden. Sin is the burden, not obedience. And justification and sanctification are not the same. One is the gift that saves us. The other is the fruit that proves we belong to Him.

With these truths in place, we can now look at the verses people most often use to claim Torah ended and see each one in its full context.

Ephesians 2:15 - Did Yeshua Abolish the Law?

The Claim: Paul says the Law was abolished at the cross.

The Verse (NLT):
Ephesians 2:15
"He did this by ending the system of law with its commandments and regulations. He made peace between Jews and Gentiles by creating in Himself one new people from the two groups."

Many read this as "Jesus abolished the Torah."
But Paul is not talking about the Torah.

The phrase "system of law with its commandments and regulations" translates a Greek word: dogma.

Dogma refers to:

THE RISE OF MARCION AND THE FALL OF THE FAITHFUL

- man made decrees
- social barriers
- purity rules created by the Pharisees
- traditions of the elders

It NEVER refers to the Torah of God in Scripture.

Paul's point is simple. Yeshua removed the human traditions that kept Jews and Gentiles apart. He did not abolish God's commandments.

Let's read Paul's own clarification only a few chapters later.

Ephesians 6:2–3 (NLT):
"Honor your father and mother. This is the first commandment with a promise. If you honor your father and mother, things will go well for you."

Paul quotes the Torah as authoritative after Ephesians 2:15.
He has not abolished anything God wrote.

Romans 10:4 - "Christ is the end of the Law"

The Claim: Jesus ended the Law.

The Verse (NKJV):
Romans 10:4
"For Christ is the end of the law for righteousness to everyone who believes."

This is one of the most misinterpreted verses in the entire Bible. The key issue is the word "end." In Greek, Paul uses the word τέλος (*telos*). That word does not mean the abolishing of something or the canceling of it. *Telos* speaks of the goal, the aim, the intended target, the purpose for which something exists. It can refer to fulfillment or completion, but never in the sense of discarding what led you there. Even when *telos* carries the idea of "terminate," it means the reaching of a goal, not the destruction of the thing itself. Paul's point is simple. Yeshua is the purpose the Torah has been aiming toward from the beginning. He embodies it, reveals it, and brings its meaning to its intended fullness. He does not put it away. He completes what it pointed to.

A better paraphrase would be:
"Messiah is the goal toward which the Torah points."

Paul uses the same word in 1 Timothy 1:5.

1 Timothy 1:5 (NKJV):
"Now the purpose (telos) of the commandment is love from a pure heart."

Telos = the aim.

Romans 10:4 does not teach that Torah ended. It teaches that Messiah is the One Torah leads us to. Torah points to Him. He fulfills its promises. He shows its fullness.

If Paul meant "abolish," he would not have written this only seven chapters earlier:

Romans 3:31 (NKJV):
"Do we then make void the law through faith? Certainly not. On the contrary, we establish the law."

Paul does not contradict himself.
Faith establishes the Torah.
Messiah fulfills the Torah.
Neither of those statements abolish it.

THE RISE OF MARCION AND THE FALL OF THE FAITHFUL

Colossians 2:14 - "Nailed to the Cross"

The Claim: God nailed the Torah to the cross.

The Verse (NLT):
Colossians 2:14
"He canceled the record of the charges against us and took it away by nailing it to the cross."

Many assume the "record of the charges" means the Torah itself. But Paul uses a very specific Greek word: cheirographon.

Cheirographon means:
- a handwritten record of debt
- a certificate of guilt
- a legal indictment
- an IOU acknowledging penalty

It never means "Torah."
It never means "commandments."
It always means "the list of charges proving our guilt."

The Torah is not our enemy.
Sin is our enemy.
The charges that condemned us were nailed to the cross, not the commandments of God.

If the Torah had been nailed to the cross, Paul would never say this:

Romans 7:12 (NLT):
"But still, the law itself is holy, and its commands are holy and right and good."

The Torah was not removed.
The penalty was removed.

THE RISE OF MARCION AND THE FALL OF THE FAITHFUL

Galatians 3:10-13 - The Curse

The Claim: The Law is a curse.

The Passage (NLT):
Galatians 3:10
"But those who depend on the law to make them right with God are under His curse, for the Scriptures say, 'Cursed is everyone who does not observe and obey all the commands that are written in God's Book of the Law.'"

Galatians 3:11
"So it is clear that no one can be made right with God by trying to keep the law. For the Scriptures say, 'It is through faith that a righteous person has life.'"

Galatians 3:13
"But Christ has rescued us from the curse pronounced by the law. When He was hung on the cross, He took upon Himself the curse for our wrongdoing."

Many people read this passage as if Paul were saying "the Law is a curse." But Paul never says that. Not once. The curse does not come from the Torah. The curse comes from breaking the Torah. Paul's argument is simple. If someone tries to rely on perfect law-keeping as the basis of salvation, they place themselves under a curse because no one has perfectly obeyed. And the Torah itself declares a curse upon disobedience. That is why Messiah came. He stepped into our place and bore the curse that belonged to us.

Paul is not attacking the Torah. He is attacking the false idea that salvation comes through works. He makes it clear that salvation comes through faith. The curse is the penalty for sin. It is never the

THE RISE OF MARCION AND THE FALL OF THE FAITHFUL

Torah. The Torah reveals sin. Messiah removes sin. Both truths stand together, and neither cancels the other.

Galatians 4:21-31 - Hagar and Sarah

The Claim: The Law is slavery and must be cast out.

The Passage (NLT Excerpts):
Galatians 4:24
"These two women serve as an illustration of God's two covenants."

Galatians 4:30
"Get rid of the slave and her son."

Some read this as "cast out the Torah."
But that is not Paul's point.

Paul uses a rabbinic teaching method called midrashic allegory.
He is not assigning Hagar or Sarah to the commandments themselves.
He is describing two ways of seeking righteousness:

Hagar represents:

- trying to enter the covenant by human effort
- seeking justification through the flesh
- man-made conversion requirements
- self-righteousness

Sarah represents:

- righteousness through faith
- the promise
- God's supernatural work
- the Spirit

THE RISE OF MARCION AND THE FALL OF THE FAITHFUL

Paul is attacking legalism, not obedience.

Paul is attacking self-righteousness, not the Torah.

If Paul believed Torah obedience was slavery, he would never write this:

Romans 7:22 (NKJV):
"For I delight in the law of God according to the inward man."

The bondage in Galatians is not Torah.
The bondage is relying on the flesh instead of faith.

Acts 15 - The Four Requirements for Gentiles

The Claim: Gentiles only need four laws.

The Passage (NLT):
Acts 15:19–20
"And so my judgment is that we should not make it difficult for the Gentiles who are turning to God. Instead, we should write and tell them to abstain from eating food offered to idols, from sexual immorality, from eating the meat of strangled animals, and from consuming blood."

Many conclude that these four instructions replaced the Torah.
But that is not what Acts 15 teaches.

The question the apostles were answering was simple:

Do Gentiles need to convert to Judaism to be saved?

The answer was no.
They do not need circumcision as a salvation requirement.
They do not need to become Jews first.

THE RISE OF MARCION AND THE FALL OF THE FAITHFUL

So the apostles gave four immediate instructions so Gentiles could have table fellowship with Jewish believers. These instructions come directly from Leviticus 17–18, the laws for the sojourner dwelling among Israel.

After these instructions are given, James explains the expectation for growth.

Acts 15:21 (NLT):
"For these laws of Moses have been preached in Jewish synagogues in every city on every Sabbath for many generations."

James assumes Gentiles will be learning the Torah every Sabbath as they worship with the community.

Acts 15 does not abolish Torah.
It establishes the doorway into it.

Acts 10 - "Rise, Peter... Kill and eat"

The Claim: God abolished the food laws.

This is one of the most misquoted passages in the New Testament. Let's examine it carefully.

The Verses (NLT):
Acts 10:13–14
"Then a voice said to him, 'Get up, Peter. Kill and eat.'
'No, Lord,' Peter declared. 'I have never eaten anything that our Jewish laws have declared impure or unclean.'"

Peter refuses the command.
Years after the resurrection.
Years after Pentecost.
Filled with the Holy Spirit.

THE RISE OF MARCION AND THE FALL OF THE FAITHFUL

If Yeshua had abolished food laws in Mark 7, Peter did not know. And notice the obvious point:

Peter does not say,
"Thank God Jesus already declared all foods clean."

Instead he says,
"I have never eaten anything unclean."

He refuses.
Three times.

After the vision, Peter gives the interpretation.

Acts 10:28 (CJB):
"God has shown me that I should not call any person common or unclean."

The vision is not about food.
It is about people.

And the Greek text confirms it.

Peter uses two words:

- koinos - man made impurity
- akathartos - biblical impurity

Peter had absorbed traditions that called Gentiles "common." God corrected him.

The vision breaks down human barriers, not divine commandments.

Then the Spirit falls on Gentiles to prove the point.

Nothing in Acts 10 changes the food laws.
Everything in Acts 10 changes how Peter views Gentiles.

THE RISE OF MARCION AND THE FALL OF THE FAITHFUL

Romans 14 - "Let each be fully convinced"

The Claim: Romans 14 proves that food laws no longer matter.

The Verse:
Romans 14:14 (NLT):
"I know and am convinced on the authority of the Lord Jesus that no food, in and of itself, is wrong to eat. But if someone believes it is wrong, then for that person it is wrong."

This chapter is often used to suggest that Paul does not care what believers eat.
But Romans 14 is not a chapter about food laws.
It is a chapter about personal opinions, not God's commandments.

Paul states his subject clearly:
Romans 14:1 (NLT):
"Accept other believers who are weak in faith and do not argue with them about what they think is right or wrong."

The Greek word for "opinions" is dialogismōn, which means personal reasoning or private preferences.
Paul is not discussing the commands of God.
He is dealing with disputes over private convictions within the Roman congregations.

What was the argument actually about?

The believers in Rome were wrestling with two main issues:

1. Eating meat sold in marketplaces that may have been offered to idols

2. Vegetarianism as a safety measure against unknowingly eating such meat

This has nothing to do with clean versus unclean animals.
Paul never mentions pork, shellfish, or anything defined as unclean in the Torah.

Paul's concern is that believers stop judging each other over gray areas where Scripture does not directly command or forbid.

Paul's central point

Romans 14:14 (NLT):
"I know and am convinced on the authority of the Lord Jesus that no food, in and of itself, is wrong to eat. But if someone believes it is wrong, then for that person it is wrong."

The phrase "in and of itself" refers to foods already permitted by God.
Paul is not saying that a believer's opinion can override Torah.
He is saying that clean food is still clean even if it passed through a pagan market.

Paul upholds the food laws

Notice what Paul does not say.
He never says:

"God has cleansed all animals."
"Nothing is unclean anymore."
"Eat whatever you want."

Instead, he anchors everything in Torah categories.

THE RISE OF MARCION AND THE FALL OF THE FAITHFUL

Romans 14:20 (NLT):
"Remember, all foods are acceptable, but it is wrong to eat something if it makes another person stumble."

"All foods" refers to foods defined by Scripture as food.
Unclean animals were never considered food in biblical language.
They were never described with the Greek word broma.
Paul uses broma here, not kreas (generic meat).
He is speaking about lawful foods.

Paul's real concern

Avoid using your freedom to harm a brother or sister.

That is the heart of the chapter.
Not diet.
Not abolishing Torah.
Not redefining food.

Paul ends the chapter by appealing to conscience and community love.

Romans 14:23 (NLT):
"But if you have doubts about whether or not you should eat something, you are sinning if you go ahead and do it."

He never cancels the food laws.
He teaches believers how to walk in love while keeping them.

1 Timothy 4:1-5 - "Every creature of God is good"

The Claim: All animals are now acceptable to eat.

The Verse:
1 Timothy 4:5 (NLT):

THE RISE OF MARCION AND THE FALL OF THE FAITHFUL

"Since everything God created is good, we should not reject any of it but receive it with thanks.
For we know it is made acceptable by the word of God and prayer."

Let's look at the passage.

1 Timothy 4:1–5 (NLT):
"Now the Holy Spirit tells us clearly that in the last times some will turn away from the true faith. They will follow deceptive spirits and teachings that come from demons.
These people are hypocrites and liars.
They forbid people to marry, and they require them to abstain from certain foods that God created to be received with thanks by those who believe and know the truth.
Since everything God created is good, we should not reject any of it but receive it with thanks.
For we know it is made acceptable by the word of God and prayer."

Several parts of this passage are misunderstood.

1. The issue is "forbidding" food that God created to be received
Paul is rebuking a false ascetic movement that banned:

- Marriage
- fasting from foods God approved
- unnecessary self-denial

The key phrase is this:

"foods that God created to be received."

God did not create all animals to be eaten.
Genesis 1 to 2 shows humans originally eating plants.
Genesis 7 shows clean and unclean animals long before Moses.

THE RISE OF MARCION AND THE FALL OF THE FAITHFUL

Leviticus 11 defines which animals God created to be received with thanksgiving.

Paul is defending God's created order.
Not altering it.

2. "Everything God created is good" refers to creation, not diet
Paul is teaching against the idea that physical creation is evil.
This was a Gnostic idea.

He is not saying,
"Everything God created is food."

He is saying,
"Everything God created is good."

These are not the same thing.

3. "Made acceptable by the word of God and prayer" has a limiting qualifier
The phrase "word of God" refers to the Scriptures.
What the Scriptures declare as food is received with prayer.
Prayer does not transform forbidden animals into food.

Paul cannot contradict God's own Torah.
He cannot contradict Yeshua's sinless obedience.
He cannot contradict his own statements in Romans 7.

Paul is rebuking false religion.
Not rewriting Leviticus.

Titus 1:15 - "To the pure, all things are pure"

The Claim: Torah food laws no longer matter because everything is pure now.

THE RISE OF MARCION AND THE FALL OF THE FAITHFUL

The verse:
Titus 1:15 (NLT):
"Everything is pure to those whose hearts are pure. But nothing is pure to those who are corrupt and unbelieving, because their minds and consciences are corrupted."

Paul is not talking about food.
He is talking about hearts.

The context is false teachers adding man-made rules.
This is the same issue Yeshua confronted in Matthew 15.

Paul's point is simple.
Those who are pure will live in purity.
Those who are corrupt will corrupt everything they touch.

Paul is not overturning the distinction in Leviticus.
He is contrasting two kinds of people.

Hebrews 8 - "A new covenant"

The Claim: The New Covenant means the Torah is abolished.

The Verse:
Hebrews 8:8 (NLT)
"But when God found fault with the people, He said:
'The day is coming, says the Lord, when I will make a new covenant with the people of Israel and Judah.'"

The author of Hebrews quotes Jeremiah 31.
But look at what God actually promises.

Hebrews 8:10 (NLT):
"But this is the new covenant I will make with the people of Israel

THE RISE OF MARCION AND THE FALL OF THE FAITHFUL

on that day, says the Lord. I will put My laws in their minds, and I will write them on their hearts."

The New Covenant does not abolish the Torah.
It relocates it.

It moves the commandments from stone tablets into the human heart by the Spirit.

Under the Old Covenant:
The Torah was written on stone
The people's hearts were hard

Under the New Covenant:
The Torah is written on our hearts
The Spirit empowers obedience

The fault was never the Torah.
It was the people.

The New Covenant strengthens obedience.
It does not silence it.

Chapter 30 Marcion in New Clothes: A Rebuttal to Dispensationalism

There are few doctrines in the modern Church that have shaped people's reading of Scripture as deeply as Dispensationalism. It sounds harmless at first. Neat charts. Seven ages. Clean dividing lines. But once you start following the logic, you see how easy it becomes to separate the God of the "Old Testament" from the God of the "New Testament." You see how quickly people begin talking like there were two peoples of God, two covenants, two gospels, and two paths of obedience.

This appendix is not written to win a fight. It is written to help believers see clearly again. Scripture has one God. One Gospel. One covenant line. One Messiah. One people of God. One way of salvation through every generation. The moment we forget that, we step back into the shadow of Marcion.

---

1. The Myth of the "Old Testament God vs New Testament God"

One of the oldest and most destructive ideas in Dispensationalism is the belief that God acted one way in the Old Testament and behaves differently in the New. People rarely say it outright, but it shows up in the way they talk about Scripture. They picture the God of the Old Testament as stern, strict, and ready to judge, while the God revealed in Yeshua is gentle, patient, and eager to forgive. Once that idea settles in the heart, people begin to choose which version of God they like better.

THE RISE OF MARCION AND THE FALL OF THE FAITHFUL

When you trace this belief to its roots, you discover it is not new at all. Marcion taught the same thing in the second century. He claimed the God of Israel was angry and inferior, and that Jesus came to reveal a better God. He insisted the two could not be reconciled, so he simply cut out the entire Old Testament and removed most of the Gospels. He did not want the God of Israel, so he created a softer deity to replace Him.

Dispensationalism does not go that far, but it leans in the same direction. It subtly tells believers that there was one way God ruled in the past and another way He rules today. It suggests grace began with the New Testament and law belonged to a former age. It paints the Father as strict and Yeshua as merciful, as if the Son must shield us from the Father's severity. The moment you accept this division, your entire view of God becomes fractured.

But Scripture does not present two different Gods. Scripture reveals one God who has always been the same. Every time you hear someone say, "God was strict back then," or "Jesus changed how God deals with people," you are hearing a modern echo of Marcion's error.

Now look at what God says about Himself.

Malachi 3:6 (NLT):
"I am the Lord, and I do not change."

Those nine words dismantle the entire claim.
If God does not change, His character does not change.
His expectations do not change.
His definition of righteousness does not change.
His compassion, justice, mercy, warnings, and promises all flow from the same heart.

THE RISE OF MARCION AND THE FALL OF THE FAITHFUL

Yeshua makes the same point about His relationship with the Father.

John 5:19 (NLT):
"I tell you the truth, the Son can do nothing by Himself. He does only what He sees the Father doing."

Yeshua is not a new version of God.
He is the Father made visible.
Whatever He does, the Father is doing.
Whatever He teaches, the Father teaches.
Whatever mercy He shows, the Father is showing.

If Yeshua forgives sinners in the New Testament, it is because the Father forgave sinners in the Old.
If Yeshua calls people to repentance, it is because the Father called people to repentance from the beginning.
If Yeshua heals the brokenhearted, restores the outcast, and shows compassion to the humble, then this has always been the heart of God.

Every act of mercy in the Gospels is a window into the Father's heart in the Torah.

Dispensationalism tries to divide God into two modes.
Scripture will not allow it.

The God who walked with Adam is the same God who walked among us in Yeshua.
The God who thundered from Sinai is the same God who whispered in Galilee.
The God who judged Egypt is the same God who healed the leper.
The God who spoke through Moses is the same God who taught in the Temple courts.

THE RISE OF MARCION AND THE FALL OF THE FAITHFUL

The God who promised a new covenant is the same God who poured out His Spirit in Acts.

There is no before and after in God's character.
There is only consistency, continuity, and covenant faithfulness.

This is why any teaching that separates the God of the Old Testament from the God of the New is not biblical. It is Marcionism retold with nicer vocabulary and modern charts.

---

2. The Artificial Split Between Israel and the Church

One of the core ideas in many versions of Dispensationalism is that Israel and the Church are two different peoples with two different destinies. According to this view, God had His plan for Israel in the Old Testament, and then He began a brand new program called "the Church Age" after the resurrection. Israel was earthly. The Church is heavenly. Israel was about law. The Church is about grace. Israel had promises. The Church has something else. Once you swallow that idea, the whole Bible divides into two competing stories.

This claim sounds tidy at first, but Scripture never speaks this way. You will not find a single prophet, apostle, or teacher in the entire Bible who describes two peoples of God. Instead, you see covenant language that runs from Genesis to Revelation with remarkable unity. God says He has one flock, one Shepherd, one covenant line, one olive tree, and one kingdom. Every time Dispensationalism tries to split God's people into separate groups, it has to cut against the grain of Scripture to do it.

THE RISE OF MARCION AND THE FALL OF THE FAITHFUL

What makes this even more concerning is how much this resembles Marcion's old idea. Marcion said the followers of Jesus were a brand new people who had no connection to Israel at all. He claimed the God of the Hebrew Scriptures had abandoned Israel, and Jesus came to reveal a different God with a different plan. Replace Marcion's wording with modern terms, and you hear the same pattern. One plan for Israel, a different plan for the Church. One covenant for Israel, a different covenant for Christians. One identity for Israel, another identity for believers today.

The names and timelines may change, but the idea is the same. It separates what God joined together. It tells Gentile believers they are something other than God's historic covenant people. It also strips Israel of her own calling by claiming God has moved on to something better. Scripture does not allow either conclusion. The moment you divide Israel and the Church, the story of the Bible loses its connection, its continuity, and its covenant heart.

Now see how plainly Scripture speaks.

Paul could not be clearer.

Romans 11:17 (NLT):
"But you who were branches from a wild olive tree have been grafted in."

Gentile believers are not planted in a new tree.
We are not a replacement tree.
We do not form our own tree.
We are wild branches grafted into Israel's cultivated tree.

Paul continues with equal force.

THE RISE OF MARCION AND THE FALL OF THE FAITHFUL

Romans 11:24 (NLT):
"For if God was willing to do something contrary to nature by grafting you into a cultivated tree, He will be far more eager to graft the original branches back into the tree where they belong."

One tree.
One root.
One people of God.

Yeshua teaches the same truth.

John 10:16 (NLT):
"I have other sheep, too, that are not of this sheepfold. I must bring them also. They will listen to My voice, and there will be one flock and one Shepherd."

Yeshua does not say there will be two flocks or two programs.
He says one flock under one Shepherd.

Dispensationalism splits what Scripture unites.
Marcion attempted the same division.
The apostles confronted it in their day.
We must confront it in ours.

3. The Claim That Torah Belonged to a Different "Dispensation"

A common belief within Dispensationalism is that the Torah was only for ancient Israel and belonged to a past age God has now closed. According to this view, the commandments were temporary, tied to a former dispensation, and set aside once

THE RISE OF MARCION AND THE FALL OF THE FAITHFUL

Yeshua came. People say things like, "That was for the Jews," or, "We are in the Church Age now," or, "The Law ended at the cross."

At first, this seems harmless. It offers a simple chart with clean boundaries. But if you think it through, the entire Bible starts to break apart. If Torah only belonged to another age, then righteousness changes with time. Holiness changes with time. The definition of sin changes with time. The meaning of obedience changes with time. What pleased God in one era supposedly displeases Him in another. That is not the God of Scripture. That is not the God who says He does not change.

And once again, this idea does not come from the prophets or the apostles. It comes from Marcion's old belief that the Torah was the product of a lesser god and had nothing to do with followers of Jesus. Marcion said Torah belonged to a different deity and a different world. Dispensationalism says Torah belonged to a different dispensation and a different people. The packaging is different, but the message is the same. Both systems remove the Torah from the life of God's people.

But when you read the prophets, you see a very different picture. Far from saying Torah would end, they say God would restore His people and empower them to walk in His commandments. They do not look backward to a fading era. They look forward to a renewed covenant where obedience flows from a transformed heart.

Listen to Jeremiah.

Jeremiah 31:33 (NLT):
"But this is the new covenant I will make with the people of Israel on that day, says the Lord. I will put My instructions deep within them, and I will write them on their hearts."

THE RISE OF MARCION AND THE FALL OF THE FAITHFUL

Dispensationalism says the New Covenant removes the Torah.
Jeremiah says the New Covenant moves the Torah inside of us.

The prophet Ezekiel says the same thing.

Ezekiel 36:27 (NLT):
"And I will put My Spirit in you so that you will follow My decrees and be careful to obey My regulations."

The Spirit does not replace obedience.
The Spirit empowers obedience.

This is the exact opposite of what Dispensationalism teaches. The prophets tell us that a time is coming when God will renew His people, transform their hearts, and place His commands within them so they can walk in His ways with joy. That is the New Covenant.

This is not a different dispensation.
This is the same God fulfilling the same promises by the same Spirit.

Torah is not the old life.
Torah is the fruit of the new life.

A new heart does not reject God's ways.
A new heart delights in them.

The moment we treat the Torah as a relic from another age, we step into Marcion's shadow. The moment we see Torah as a gift written on the heart by the Spirit, we step into the New Covenant for what it truly is.

THE RISE OF MARCION AND THE FALL OF THE FAITHFUL

4. The Claim That Yeshua Gave a New Religion

Many dispensational teachers speak as if Yeshua came to introduce Christianity.
But Yeshua never used that word.
The apostles never used that word.
The early believers never used that word.

They called themselves something else.

Acts 24:14 (NLT):
"I follow the Way, which they call a cult. I worship the God of our ancestors, and I firmly believe the Jewish law and everything written in the prophets."

Paul says plainly that he follows the Torah and the Prophets.
This is the same Paul many claim abolished them.

Yeshua Himself said:

Matthew 5:17 (NLT):
"Don't misunderstand why I have come. I did not come to abolish the law of Moses or the writings of the prophets. No, I came to accomplish their purpose."

Yeshua is not starting something new.
He is fulfilling something ancient.

Dispensationalism asks us to believe that the Messiah of Israel came to abolish the faith of Israel.
Scripture shows the opposite.

THE RISE OF MARCION AND THE FALL OF THE FAITHFUL

5. The Idea That Yeshua Preached Only to Jews

Dispensationalism often says that Yeshua's teachings were for Jews, but Paul's teachings were for the Gentiles. This is how they create the divide between law and grace. But the Gospels tell a different story.

Yeshua told the Great Commission.

Matthew 28:19–20 (NLT):
"Therefore, go and make disciples of all the nations.
Teach these new disciples to obey all the commands I have given you."

What commands?
His commands.
Not a new set of teachings for Gentiles.
Not a replacement covenant.

The same words He taught in Judea and Galilee He commands us to teach to the nations.

Yeshua also ministered beyond Israel during His earthly life:

- The Samaritan woman
- The Roman centurion
- The Syrophoenician woman
- The Gerasene man
- The Greeks who sought Him before Passover

Yeshua did not preach two gospels.
He preached one kingdom to all people.

THE RISE OF MARCION AND THE FALL OF THE FAITHFUL

6. The Belief That Paul Preached a Different Gospel

Some forms of Dispensationalism go much further than dividing Israel and the Church. They claim that the Gospel itself did not begin until Paul. According to these teachers, everything Yeshua preached during His earthly ministry belonged to another age, another dispensation, another group of people. They say the Sermon on the Mount, the parables, the kingdom teachings, the call to repentance, the warnings, and even the Great Commission were all "Old Testament" material. In their view, the true Gospel only arrived with Paul's letters.

Once you accept this idea, everything collapses. Yeshua's words become optional. His commandments become irrelevant. His teachings are treated like relics from a previous era God supposedly closed. People begin to say things like, "Jesus was talking to Jews, not us," or, "The cross started a brand new religion Paul understood better than Jesus." With one sweep of the hand, the heart of the New Covenant gets shoved into a category labeled "For Israel only," while Paul's letters are elevated above Yeshua Himself.

This is not just bad theology. This is a return to Marcion. Marcion tried to cut out the Gospels and keep only a trimmed version of Luke. Modern versions of this doctrine do the same thing. They may not remove pages from the Bible, but they strip Yeshua's words of authority. If Yeshua's message was not the Gospel, then believers are left with a Messiah who did not preach the Good News and disciples who followed Him without ever hearing it. That picture does not come from Scripture. It comes from a man-made system.

Now we contrast this with what Scripture actually says.

THE RISE OF MARCION AND THE FALL OF THE FAITHFUL

Paul himself rejected the idea that he preached something new, different, or separate from what Yeshua taught.

Galatians 1:8 (NLT):
"Let God's curse fall on anyone, including us or even an angel from heaven, who preaches a different kind of Good News than the one we preached to you."

Paul says there is only one Gospel.
Not one for Jews and another for Gentiles.
Not one for before the cross and another after.
Not one for Jesus and another for Paul.

He continues.

Galatians 1:11–12 (NLT):
"Dear brothers and sisters, I want you to understand that the gospel message I preach is not based on mere human reasoning.
I received my message from no human source.
I received it by direct revelation from Jesus Christ."

Paul is not correcting Yeshua.
He is not replacing Yeshua.
He is preaching the same message Yeshua gave him.

Yeshua Himself confirms this unity.

John 17:20–21 (NLT):
"I am praying not only for these disciples but also for all who will ever believe in Me through their message.
I pray that they will all be one, just as You and I are one."

One body.
One faith.
One Gospel.

THE RISE OF MARCION AND THE FALL OF THE FAITHFUL

Dispensationalism asks us to believe that Yeshua preached to Jews while Paul preached the "real" gospel to Gentiles. Scripture shows that both preached one kingdom, one Messiah, one salvation, and one call to obey God.

---

7. Dispensationalism Is Marcionism in a New Suit

There is a story most of us heard as children called *The Emperor's New Clothes*. You know how it goes. A pair of smooth-talking tailors convinced the emperor they had woven a special garment that only the wise could see. No one wanted to look foolish, so everyone pretended. The king pretended. His servants pretended. The crowd pretended. The whole kingdom went along with the illusion until finally a child, free from the pressure to impress anyone, said the simple truth out loud. "He is not wearing anything at all."

Dispensationalism often works the same way. It comes wrapped in impressive charts and complex timelines. It is presented with academic vocabulary and confident explanations. People nod not because they understand it, but because they assume someone else does. Entire congregations go along because they do not want to be the one person who says, "Wait a minute. That does not line up with Scripture."

But when you peel away the layers and look at the core claims, something becomes painfully obvious. Dispensationalism is not wearing anything new. It is the same old outfit Marcion stitched together almost two thousand years ago. The terminology is updated. The presentation is cleaner. But the fabric is the same.

THE RISE OF MARCION AND THE FALL OF THE FAITHFUL

Marcion was the first to draw a line between the "God of the Old Testament" and the "God of the New." Dispensationalism follows that line. Marcion separated Israel from the followers of Yeshua. Dispensationalism does the same. Marcion threw out the Torah as a relic of a former age. Dispensationalism labels it a different dispensation. Marcion elevated Paul over Yeshua. Dispensationalism does that quietly by using Paul to cancel the words of Yeshua.

Different tailors. Same garment.

And just like the emperor in the story, what the Church needs most is honesty. We need the courage to say what becomes obvious the moment we stop pretending. The suit is not real. The so-called "dispensations" are not in the Bible. The division it creates between Israel and the Church, between law and grace, between the Father and the Son, does not come from the apostles. It comes from a system that Scripture never taught.

Marcion rejected the God of the Old Testament.
Dispensationalism separates Him from the God of the New.

Marcion cut away the Torah.
Dispensationalism sets it aside as a relic of a closed era.

Marcion rejected Israel.
Dispensationalism replaces Israel with a second people of God.

Marcion claimed Paul preached a different gospel.
Dispensationalism uses Paul's letters to silence the teachings of Yeshua.

The packaging may change.
The vocabulary may shift.

THE RISE OF MARCION AND THE FALL OF THE FAITHFUL

The presentation may feel more polished.
But underneath, the ideas remain the same.

Every time the Church divides Scripture into categories that God Himself never created, we take a step onto Marcion's old path. When we separate the God of the "Old Testament" from the God of the "New," or when we split the Bible into law versus grace, Israel versus the Church, or Torah versus the Gospel, we are not walking in apostolic teaching. We are reviving a heresy the early Church already refuted.

Scripture calls us back to something beautifully simple.

There is one God who never changes.
One Messiah who fulfills every promise He made.
One Spirit who empowers His people to walk in obedience.
One people who are grafted into the same root.
One covenant written not on stone, but on willing hearts.
One Gospel preached by Yeshua and confirmed by Paul.
One faith delivered once for all.

The sooner we let Scripture speak for itself, the sooner the fog lifts and the truth becomes clear again. May the whole Church return to what God has said from the very beginning.

THE RISE OF MARCION AND THE FALL OF THE FAITHFUL

About The Author

Jeff Brannon hails from the Piney Woods of Northeast Texas, along the shores of Caddo Lake. He surrendered his life to Christ at fifteen and has faithfully served in ministry for over 36 years. His journey has taken him from Youth Pastor and Evangelist to a four-year tenure as Senior Pastor of Caddo Lake Church in Uncertain, Texas ... the very congregation where he first encountered Jesus as Lord.

Driven by a passion for biblical teaching and apologetics, Jeff delights in helping others understand and defend their faith. Together with his wife, Miranda, he leads The Way Remnant - an online ministry reaching audiences on YouTube, Facebook, TikTok, X, and Rumble. They also provide marriage counseling and host regular gatherings in their West Virginia home.

Connect with Jeff and Miranda at TheWayRemnant@gmail.com.

Visit our website:

TheWayRemnant.com

See us on YouTube:
http://YouTube.com/TheWayRemnant

THE RISE OF MARCION AND THE FALL OF THE FAITHFUL

Check out these other books by Jeff:

THE RISE OF MARCION AND THE FALL OF THE FAITHFUL

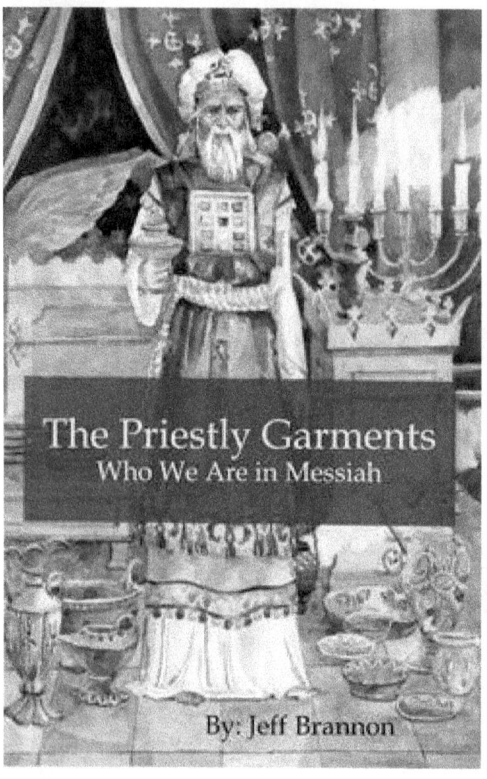

The Priestly Garments: Who We Are in Messiah
A Thirty - Year Exploration of Levitical Divine Vestments

Dive into a lifetime of discovery as you explore the sacred attire prescribed in Leviticus - garments that reveal not only the ancient world of Israel's tabernacle but also the heart of Messiah's work on our behalf. What began as a spark of curiosity at a Wednesday night youth service has grown into a comprehensive study of Hebrew language, Near Eastern culture, and biblical typology, offering fresh insights on every fold of the priestly robes.

Why This Book Matters

Each chapter walks you through the original Hebrew terms and cultural contexts, illuminating how every color, thread count, and gemstone speaks of promises purchased at Calvary. You'll see how a pastor's teenage fascination became a scholarly pilgrimage, culminating in layered commentary that bridges ancient ritual and modern devotion.

Equip Yourself for Deeper Study
 Whether you're a student of Scripture, a teacher in the church, or someone longing for intimacy with the Creator, these pages will become a roadmap for encountering God's design "from the very beginning." Let the priestly garments clothe your understanding - opening doors to richer worship, profound healing, and unshakeable identity in Messiah.

Claim the truths woven into every stitch and stand fortified by the promises our Creator ordained before time began.

THE RISE OF MARCION AND THE FALL OF THE FAITHFUL

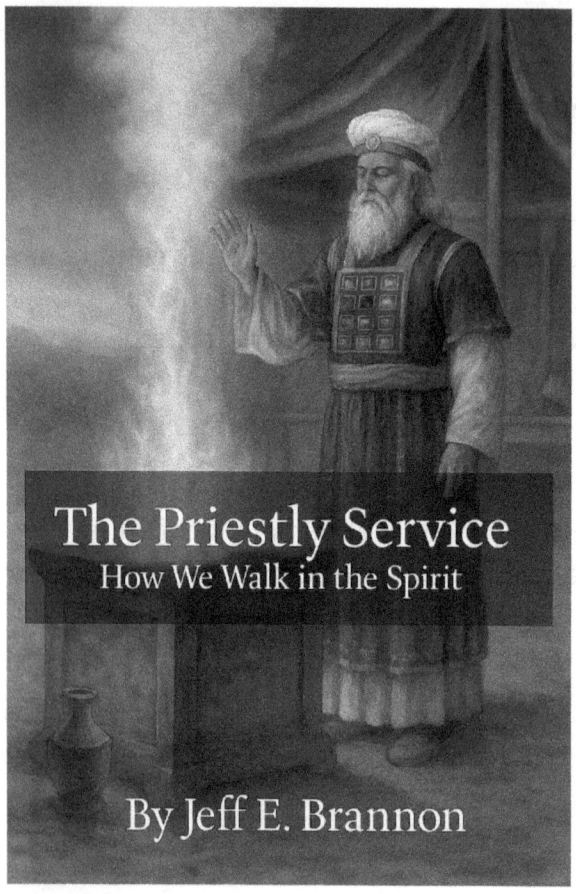

The Priestly Service: How We Walk in the Spirit
A Study of Levitical Duty, Worship, and Kingdom Identity

Step beyond the garments and into the work. This volume follows the path from vestments to vocation, from being clothed in righteousness to living as those who minister before the King. Where **The Priestly Garments** explored identity, **The Priestly Service** explores responsibility. The text draws from Torah, Temple history, and the lives of the priests themselves to reveal how service shapes the soul, forms the community, and calls us into a life of daily worship.

THE RISE OF MARCION AND THE FALL OF THE FAITHFUL

Why This Book Matters

Here you trace the rhythm of priestly duty through sacrifice, incense, intercession, and blessing. You see how ancient service patterns mirror the life of a believer who walks by the Spirit. Each chapter unpacks Hebrew terminology and historical practice, showing how the Levitical blueprint still pulses beneath New Covenant faith. You learn not only what the priests did, but why it still matters for anyone who seeks to live holy, love well, and stand as a living tabernacle before Yehovah.

Equip Yourself to Serve

If you hunger for deeper obedience, clearer purpose, and a faith expressed through action, this study will guide your steps. You move from the holy place to the most holy place, from ritual to renewal. You discover how prayer becomes incense, how service becomes worship, and how obedience becomes joy. This is a call to rise as priests in Messiah, offering your life as a continual offering of praise.

Step into the temple. Take up the service. Walk in the Spirit with boldness and wonder.

THE RISE OF MARCION AND THE FALL OF THE FAITHFUL

Book 1 of The Watcher's Trilogy

Before Adam: The Fall of Enlil is a gripping theological novel that dares to explore the ancient war before time - a cosmic rebellion that set the stage for everything we know about good and evil, Eden and exile, heaven and earth.

Long before the creation of Adam, before the first sunrise, there was light - pure, holy, divine. And in that Light walked Enlil, a majestic angel created with brilliance, music, and purpose. But pride swelled within him. What began as a question became a challenge. What became a challenge became war.

THE RISE OF MARCION AND THE FALL OF THE FAITHFUL

This is the story of a rebellion in the heavens - a celestial uprising led not by a monster, but by one who once worshiped at the throne of Yehovah. Before Adam weaves together ancient biblical imagery, forgotten texts, and rich speculative theology to tell the story of how beauty became corruption, and how the seeds of deception were planted long before Eve ever met the serpent.

As the angels choose sides and the fabric of creation trembles, Enlil faces judgment - but not as expected. His punishment is not immediate destruction, but a deeper sentence: to witness, from the dust, the unfolding plan of redemption, mercy, and glory that he once rejected.

This book is not just fiction - it's a bold reimagining that invites readers to consider the spiritual warfare behind the veil, the justice and mercy of a holy God, and the prophetic truths embedded in the Genesis narrative.

Before Adam is perfect for readers who love theological depth, epic storytelling, and thought-provoking insights into Scripture. Whether you're a scholar, a seeker, or simply captivated by the mysteries of creation, this story will challenge what you thought you knew - and draw you into a war that still echoes today.

THE RISE OF MARCION AND THE FALL OF THE FAITHFUL

The Nephilim, A Giant Walk Through History
Book 2 of The Watcher's Trilogy

A sweeping, biblically grounded adventure that begins with Jared, Noah's grandfather, and races through history into the modern day - revealing the hidden legacy of the Nephilim, "those who fell." Born of fallen angels and human women, these giants reshape everything we thought we knew about Scripture and Earth's ancient past. Drawing on canonical texts alongside extra - biblical treasures such as 1 Enoch, Jubilees, Jasher, and the Book of Giants, this story weaves fact and fiction into a thrilling narrative that challenges the reader to ask: If God is love, why did He permit genocide in the Old Testament? What did Jesus mean when He said the end times would mirror Noah's day?

THE RISE OF MARCION AND THE FALL OF THE FAITHFUL

From the rise of Nimrod and his enigmatic queen to the mysterious Vimana described in over a thousand ancient writings, every twist of this tale springs from synchronized, historically endorsed sources including Dead Sea Scroll fragments. You'll witness monumental battles, secret technologies, and angelic councils, all set against a backdrop of real places and events that illuminate questions the modern church often fears to face.

Journey through epochs of wonder and warning, and glimpse of what the near future may hold. Are the Nephilim truly gone, or do they walk among us still? Discover the answers in this extraordinary fusion of scholarship and storytelling - where the past comes alive, the present is transformed, and the future pulses with possibility.

THE RISE OF MARCION AND THE FALL OF THE FAITHFUL

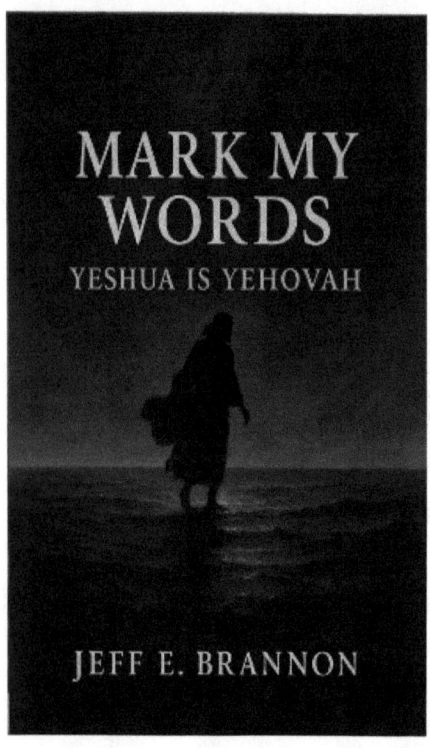

Mark My Words: Yeshua is Yehovah
Unveiling the Divine Identity in the Gospel of Mark

For generations, readers have seen the miracles and teachings of Yeshua without realizing what Mark was truly declaring: the Holy One of Israel Himself walked among His people. **In *Mark My Words: Yeshua is Yehovah***, Jeff E. Brannon takes you through the Gospel of Mark verse by verse to uncover the original revelation - Yeshua is not merely sent by Yehovah; He *is* Yehovah revealed in the flesh.

Written from a Hebraic and Spirit-filled perspective, this book restores the ancient understanding that the early believers held with certainty. Brannon shows how Mark's "simple" Gospel carries profound theological precision. Each miracle, confrontation, and

THE RISE OF MARCION AND THE FALL OF THE FAITHFUL

act of compassion mirrors Yehovah's own works recorded in the Torah and Prophets. When Yeshua commands the wind and sea, forgives sin, walks on water, and heals the leper, He displays the same authority described of Yehovah throughout Scripture.

Drawing from Hebrew language insights, early manuscript evidence, and the prophetic continuity of the Tanakh, **Mark My Words** bridges scholarship and revelation. It demonstrates how the divine name, nature, and mission of Yehovah are embodied perfectly in Yeshua the Messiah.

This study is not just informational - it's transformational. As you trace each chapter, you'll see the unity of the Father and the Son in action. You'll rediscover the covenant faithfulness of Yehovah expressed through Yeshua's mercy, holiness, and power.

Through this journey you will learn:

- How Mark's structure and language reveal Yeshua as Yehovah in human form.
- Why early followers of Messiah had no struggle affirming His divinity.
- How the Gospel narratives fulfill Yehovah's ancient promises of redemption.

Mark My Words: Yeshua is Yehovah calls you to read the Gospel with new eyes and a restored heart. When you finish, you'll not only know more about Yeshua - you'll recognize Him as the covenant - keeping God who spoke from Sinai, calmed the storm, and still calls His people by name.

Return to Mark's Gospel. Hear His voice. See His glory. Discover that Yeshua is Yehovah.

THE RISE OF MARCION AND THE FALL OF THE FAITHFUL

A Word from the Publisher

When you finish a book that speaks to your heart, your response matters more than you might think. Reviews are not just feedback; they are a way to share truth, encourage the author, and help others discover what you have found.

Online stores like Amazon use reviews and ratings to decide which books to recommend. The more readers engage, the more visibility a message receives. It is not about popularity; it is about reach. Every time you leave a review, you help the Word go farther than algorithms alone ever could.

If this book encouraged you, taught you something new, or helped you draw closer to Yehovah, please consider taking a moment to share that. Your honest review, even a few simple sentences, can lead someone else to find the same truth that touched your life.

Thank you for being part of this mission to awaken hearts, strengthen faith, and point people back to the fullness of who Yeshua is. Your voice carries farther than you realize.

How to Leave a Review on Amazon

1. Go to Amazon.com and sign in.
2. Search for the book title (for example: *The Priestly Service: How We Walk in the Spirit*).
3. Click on the book cover or title to open the product page.
4. Scroll down until you see Customer Reviews.
5. Click Write a Customer Review.
6. Choose a star rating, then share a few sentences about what you learned or enjoyed.

7. Click Submit and that's it.

It only takes a minute, but it makes a lasting impact.

Thank you for reading, for sharing, and for helping this message reach others who are searching for truth.

www.ingramcontent.com/pod-product-compliance
Lightning Source LLC
Chambersburg PA
CBHW050853160426
43194CB00011B/2133